Jean Wyllys

The LGBTQ Voice in Brazil's Parliament – Unauthorized

Ayesha Raj

ISBN: 9781779696816
Imprint: Telephasic Workshop
Copyright © 2024 Ayesha Raj.
All Rights Reserved.

Contents

Introduction: Who the Fuck Is Jean Wyllys?

From Reality TV Star to Political Icon: Jean Wyllys' Fucking Journey

Breaking Stereotypes: How a Fucking Reality TV Show Launched Wyllys' Political Career

Reality TV has long been known for its ability to captivate audiences with drama, entertainment, and sometimes even controversy. And in the case of Jean Wyllys, it served as the launching pad for his remarkable political career. But how did a reality TV show propel Wyllys from a television star to a political icon? Let's dive into the fascinating journey of breaking stereotypes and paving the way for LGBTQ representation in Brazilian politics.

The Fucking Power of Reality TV

Reality TV shows have become a global phenomenon, captivating audiences with their unfiltered portrayal of real-life experiences. These shows often expose the raw emotions, struggles, and triumphs of the participants, making viewers feel connected and emotionally invested. The popularity of reality TV lies in its ability to provide a platform for ordinary individuals to showcase their authentic selves, empowering them with newfound fame and recognition.

From Big Brother to Big Change

Jean Wyllys' journey began when he participated in the Brazilian edition of the reality TV show "Big Brother" in 2005. This groundbreaking experience allowed Wyllys to showcase his true self on a national stage, breaking stereotypes and challenging social norms. As an openly gay man, Wyllys brought LGBTQ representation to a mainstream audience, challenging prevailing prejudices and misconceptions.

An Unconventional Political Path

Wyllys leveraged his newfound fame from "Big Brother" to transition into the world of politics. While reality TV may seem like an unlikely stepping stone for a political career, Wyllys recognized the immense power it held as a platform to reach a wide audience and influence public opinion.

Destroying Stereotypes

Wyllys' participation in "Big Brother" shattered stereotypes about the LGBTQ community. Many viewers were exposed to an openly gay man who defied societal expectations and was unapologetically himself. Wyllys' authenticity and courage in front of the cameras challenged prejudiced viewpoints and helped foster greater acceptance and understanding.

Inspiring LGBTQ Individuals

By being an openly gay participant on a reality TV show, Wyllys became a source of inspiration for LGBTQ individuals across Brazil. His presence on the show demonstrated that sexual orientation does not define a person's worth or abilities. Wyllys showed LGBTQ individuals that their voices matter and that they too can aspire to hold positions of power and influence.

Elevating the Conversation

Wyllys' participation in "Big Brother" elevated the national conversation surrounding LGBTQ rights and visibility. The show provided a platform for Wyllys to share personal stories, confront stereotypes, and challenge homophobic attitudes. Through his interactions and discussions within the house, Wyllys opened the eyes and minds of millions, sparking meaningful conversations across the country.

Beyond Entertainment

Wyllys recognized that his time on "Big Brother" was not just about fame and entertainment but an opportunity to effect real change. He used his platform to draw attention to the struggles faced by the LGBTQ community, advocating for equality, and fighting against discrimination.

The Birth of a Political Icon

Wyllys' participation in "Big Brother" not only launched his political career but also laid the foundation for his future as an LGBTQ advocate. His authenticity and courage resonated with the Brazilian public, propelling him into the political arena and solidifying his status as an icon of LGBTQ representation.

A Fucking Reality, A Fucking Icon

Jean Wyllys' journey from reality TV star to political icon is a testament to the power of breaking stereotypes and challenging societal norms. His presence on the reality TV show "Big Brother" allowed him to use his fame as a platform for change, pioneering LGBTQ representation in Brazilian politics. Wyllys' story serves as an inspiration for future LGBTQ activists and reminds us of the transformative potential of popular culture in reshaping society's perceptions and values. So, let us recognize and celebrate Wyllys' fucking journey as we continue to fight for a more inclusive and accepting world.

The Fucking Importance of Representation: How Wyllys Became a Fucking LGBTQ Icon in Brazil

Representation matters. It's a simple yet powerful concept that has the ability to transform lives and shape societies. In the case of LGBTQ rights, representation is more crucial than ever. Jean Wyllys emerged as a powerful LGBTQ icon in Brazil, not simply because he was the first openly gay politician in the country, but because he fought tirelessly to ensure that the voices and experiences of the LGBTQ community were seen, heard, and valued.

Wyllys understood that visibility was key to achieving social change. By boldly stepping into the spotlight as an openly gay individual, he shattered stereotypes and challenged societal norms. He proved that being LGBTQ was not something to be ashamed of, but rather something to embrace, celebrate, and fight for.

One of the ways Wyllys used his platform to promote LGBTQ visibility was through his participation in reality TV. While some may dismiss reality TV as trivial or shallow, Wyllys saw it as an opportunity to reach a wide audience and engage in meaningful conversations about LGBTQ rights. His appearance on "Big Brother Brazil" not only catapulted him to national fame but also allowed him to connect with millions of Brazilians who may have had little exposure to LGBTQ individuals and their struggles.

Wyllys' courageous decision to come out on national television was a defining moment in his journey towards becoming an LGBTQ icon. By sharing his personal story, he humanized the LGBTQ experience and showed that love knows no bounds. His vulnerability and authenticity touched the hearts of many, making him relatable and inspiring to countless individuals who were struggling with their own identities.

Beyond public appearances, Wyllys utilized various platforms and social media channels to engage with the LGBTQ community and amplify their voices. He recognized the power of storytelling and used it as a tool to bridge the gap between communities, foster empathy, and cultivate understanding. By sharing personal anecdotes, anecdotes, and experiences, he was able to dismantle stereotypes, build empathy, and create a sense of belonging for LGBTQ individuals across Brazil.

Wyllys also understood the significance of legislative representation in the fight for LGBTQ rights. By being present in Brazil's parliament, he was able to advocate for policies that directly addressed the needs and challenges faced by the LGBTQ community. He fought tirelessly for same-sex marriage, anti-discrimination laws, and gender equality, realizing that legal recognition and protection were essential steps towards achieving full inclusion and acceptance.

In a deeply conservative political environment, Wyllys encountered numerous obstacles and faced significant pushback from homophobic politicians and religious groups. However, he remained steadfast in his commitment to fighting for LGBTQ rights and refused to back down. His resilience and unwavering dedication inspired not only the LGBTQ community but also allies and supporters from all walks of life.

Wyllys' impact as an LGBTQ icon extended far beyond Brazil's borders. His work and advocacy served as a beacon of hope and inspiration for LGBTQ individuals around the world. By challenging the status quo, breaking barriers, and pushing for progress, he proved that change was possible, even in the face of adversity.

It is undeniable that Jean Wyllys played a pivotal role in changing the narrative surrounding LGBTQ rights in Brazil. Through his visibility, courage, and determination, he became an icon for the LGBTQ community, demonstrating that representation is not only important but crucial in the fight for social justice. As Wyllys' legacy continues to inspire future generations of LGBTQ activists, his story serves as a testament to the power of one individual to create lasting change within a society.

Fighting Back: How Wyllys Used His Fucking Platform to Confront Homophobia and Transphobia

The fight against homophobia and transphobia has been at the forefront of Jean Wyllys' activism throughout his political career. Using his platform as a member of Brazil's Parliament, Wyllys has fearlessly confronted prejudice and discrimination while advocating for the rights and equality of the LGBTQ community. In this section, we will explore the strategies Wyllys employed to challenge homophobia and transphobia and the impact of his efforts in Brazil and beyond.

Understanding Homophobia and Transphobia

Before delving into Wyllys' fight against homophobia and transphobia, it is crucial to understand these forms of discrimination. Homophobia refers to the fear, hatred, or prejudice against individuals who identify as gay, lesbian, or bisexual. Transphobia, on the other hand, is the fear, hatred, or prejudice against transgender people.

Both homophobia and transphobia manifest in various ways, including verbal harassment, physical violence, social exclusion, and discriminatory practices. These forms of prejudice perpetuate a cycle of marginalization and negatively impact the mental and emotional well-being of LGBTQ individuals.

Wyllys recognized the urgent need to address these issues, and he strategically used his platform to combat homophobia and transphobia head-on.

Building Awareness and Education

One of the first steps Wyllys took in confronting homophobia and transphobia was to raise awareness and educate the public. He understood that many prejudices arise from ignorance and misinformation. Wyllys used his fucking platform to enlighten people about LGBTQ rights and foster understanding.

Through public speeches, media appearances, and community engagement, Wyllys sought to dismantle stereotypes and challenge misconceptions about homosexuality and gender identity. He openly shared his own experiences, personal stories, and struggles, humanizing the LGBTQ experience and creating empathy among those who may have held prejudiced views.

Additionally, Wyllys worked tirelessly to promote LGBTQ-inclusive education. He advocated for comprehensive sex education in schools that includes discussions on sexual orientation and gender identity. By normalizing these topics in the curriculum, Wyllys aimed to create a more inclusive and accepting society.

Legislation and Legal Protection

Another key aspect of Wyllys' fight against homophobia and transphobia was his work on legislation and legal protection for the LGBTQ community. He pushed for the enactment of laws that would safeguard the rights of LGBTQ individuals and hold perpetrators of discrimination accountable.

Wyllys advocated for the inclusion of sexual orientation and gender identity in anti-discrimination laws, ensuring protection against discrimination in employment, housing, education, and public services. He also fought for the recognition of same-sex relationships, advocating for marriage equality and equal adoption rights for LGBTQ couples.

By actively engaging in the legislative process, Wyllys effectively brought attention to the need for legal reforms that would promote equality and combat discrimination. His efforts paved the way for significant advancements in LGBTQ rights in Brazil.

Coalitions and Alliances

Recognizing the power of unity, Wyllys formed coalitions and alliances with like-minded individuals and organizations to maximize the impact of his advocacy. He collaborated with LGBTQ rights organizations, human rights activists, and progressive politicians to build a strong support network.

Wyllys understood that collective action was essential in addressing homophobia and transphobia effectively. By working together, these coalitions could amplify their voices and exert pressure on policymakers to enact positive change.

Through joint campaigns, protests, and lobbying efforts, Wyllys and his allies created a united front against homophobia and transphobia. Their joint advocacy allowed them to challenge discriminatory practices, change public opinion, and secure legislative victories.

International Engagement

In today's interconnected world, Wyllys recognized the importance of international engagement in the fight against homophobia and transphobia. He actively sought alliances with international organizations and collaborated with LGBTQ activists from around the globe.

Wyllys utilized international platforms to shed light on the challenges faced by the LGBTQ community in Brazil. He participated in conferences, summits, and forums, sharing his experiences and amplifying the voices of LGBTQ Brazilians.

By engaging with the global community, Wyllys ensured that the fight against homophobia and transphobia in Brazil was not isolated. He drew inspiration from successful LGBTQ movements worldwide and used their strategies as a catalyst for change within his own country.

Unconventional Approach: Humanizing the LGBTQ Experience

In his fight against homophobia and transphobia, Wyllys employed an unconventional yet highly effective approach - humanizing the LGBTQ experience. He understood that personal connections and empathy were powerful tools in breaking down prejudice and discrimination.

Wyllys openly shared his personal stories, highlighting the challenges he faced as a gay man and the struggles of the LGBTQ community. By putting a human face on the issue, he created a deeper understanding and connection with his audience.

His approach was unconventional because it defied the notion of political detachment. Wyllys' willingness to be vulnerable and genuine humanized not only himself but also the larger LGBTQ community. Through his authenticity, he challenged stereotypes and fostered empathy among his constituents.

Case Studies: Impact and Successes

Looking at specific case studies, we can see the impact of Wyllys' fight against homophobia and transphobia. One notable achievement was the passage of the Gender Identity Law, which enabled transgender individuals to legally change their gender without undergoing surgery or hormone therapy. Wyllys championed this law, paving the way for greater recognition and acceptance of transgender rights.

Furthermore, Wyllys' efforts were instrumental in the decriminalization of homophobia by the Brazilian Supreme Court. In a groundbreaking ruling, the court extended existing anti-discrimination laws to cover cases of homophobia and transphobia, holding perpetrators accountable for their actions.

These successes demonstrate the significant impact of Wyllys' activism and highlight the transformative power of his strategies in challenging homophobia and transphobia.

Conclusion

Jean Wyllys' fight against homophobia and transphobia has left an indelible mark on LGBTQ rights in Brazil and beyond. Through his platform as a politician, Wyllys confronted prejudice and discrimination head-on, building awareness, advocating for legislative reforms, and forming alliances.

His unconventional approach of humanizing the LGBTQ experience, along with his commitment to international engagement, has created a lasting impact in the fight for equality. Wyllys' legacy serves as an inspiration for future LGBTQ activists, illustrating the power of resilience, unity, and unwavering dedication in the face of adversity.

As Brazil continues to grapple with systemic homophobia and transphobia, Wyllys' fight remains a shining example of what can be achieved through activism, legislation, and the unwavering belief in a more inclusive and accepting society.

The Fucking Struggles of Being an Openly Gay Politician in Brazil's Conservative Fucking Political System

Being an openly gay politician in Brazil's conservative political system comes with its fair share of struggles and challenges. Jean Wyllys, a trailblazer in LGBTQ activism, experienced firsthand the obstacles and discrimination that can arise when advocating for gay rights in a society that often does not fully embrace diversity. In this section, we will explore some of the key struggles Jean Wyllys faced as an openly gay politician, shedding light on the systemic issues that he fought against.

1. The Fucking Uphill Battle: Homophobia and Prejudice

In Brazil's conservative political landscape, homophobia and prejudice against the LGBTQ community run deep. Many politicians, influenced by religious beliefs or societal biases, perpetuate discriminatory attitudes towards gay individuals. This created a hostile environment for Jean Wyllys, who faced prejudice and opposition from fellow politicians simply because of his sexual orientation.

Wyllys often encountered offensive remarks and derogatory comments from his colleagues, undermining his credibility and ability to effectively represent the LGBTQ community. These encounters were not only hurtful but also obstructed his efforts to bring about positive change for gay rights in Brazil. Despite these challenges, Wyllys remained steadfast in his advocacy, determined to challenge the deeply-rooted homophobia ingrained within Brazil's political system.

2. The Fucking Struggle for Legislative Support

Another significant struggle that Jean Wyllys faced as an openly gay politician in Brazil was the difficulty of garnering legislative support for LGBTQ rights. Though Brazil has made strides in recognizing and protecting gay rights, such as legalizing same-sex marriage in 2013, there is still a long way to go in achieving full equality.

Wyllys encountered resistance when trying to pass legislation that would further protect the rights of LGBTQ individuals. Many conservative politicians vehemently opposed measures such as anti-discrimination laws, arguing that they infringed on religious freedom or traditional family values. This lack of support from within the political system made it challenging for Wyllys to push through vital legislation beneficial to the LGBTQ community.

However, Wyllys was determined and relentless in his pursuit of justice. He used his position in parliament to raise awareness of the discrimination faced by the LGBTQ community and advocated for inclusive policies. Despite the roadblocks he faced, Wyllys managed to make significant progress in shifting public opinion and highlighting the urgent need for legislative action.

3. The Fucking Threat of Violence

Perhaps the most disturbing struggle Jean Wyllys faced was the constant threat of violence. As an openly gay politician, he became a target for homophobic individuals and hate groups who would stop at nothing to undermine his efforts and silence his voice.

Wyllys received numerous death threats throughout his career, forcing him to live in constant fear for his safety. These threats not only affected his personal life but also hindered his ability to carry out his political duties effectively. The fear of physical harm weighed heavily on him, creating a significant emotional and mental toll.

Despite the risks, Wyllys remained resilient, refusing to be silenced by the intimidation tactics of those who opposed LGBTQ rights. He continued to speak out against homophobia and violence, drawing attention to the urgent need for greater protection and security for the LGBTQ community in Brazil.

4. The Fucking Isolation and Lack of Allies

Another struggle that Jean Wyllys faced as an openly gay politician was the sense of isolation and the lack of allies within the political landscape. The conservative majority often marginalized his viewpoints and brushed aside the importance of LGBTQ rights, leaving Wyllys to fight his battles largely on his own.

Navigating the political system without a strong support network made progress even more challenging to achieve. Wyllys struggled to find fellow politicians who shared his vision and were willing to actively collaborate on LGBTQ legislation. This absence of allies further underscored the urgent need for more representation and support for LGBTQ rights in Brazil's political arena.

In Conclusion,

Jean Wyllys' journey as an openly gay politician in Brazil's conservative political system was marked by numerous struggles. Facing homophobia, prejudice, legislative obstacles, threats of violence, and limited support from his colleagues, Wyllys exhibited immense resilience and determination in his fight for LGBTQ rights.

His story serves as a reminder that progress comes with great resilience and sacrifice. While Wyllys made notable strides in advancing LGBTQ rights in Brazil, his struggles reveal the systemic challenges that LGBTQ activists continue to face worldwide.

Wyllys' courage and unwavering advocacy have inspired a new generation of LGBTQ leaders, urging them to continue pushing for equality and fighting against discrimination. His legacy serves as a constant reminder that the fight for LGBTQ rights is far from over and that progress requires consistent effort, even in the face of adversity.

The Future of LGBTQ Politics in Brazil: How Wyllys Paved the Fucking Way for Future Leaders

The courageous leadership of Jean Wyllys has paved the way for the future of LGBTQ politics in Brazil. His impactful advocacy and relentless fight for equality have inspired countless individuals to join the movement and make their voices heard. Wyllys' fearless approach to politics, despite facing adversity and death threats, has left an indelible mark on Brazil's political landscape.

Wyllys' commitment to breaking down stereotypes and challenging societal norms has been paramount in transforming public opinion and fostering acceptance. He has shown that being openly gay is not a hindrance to effective political leadership, but rather a strength that brings a unique perspective to the table. Through his activism, Wyllys has shattered the misconception that LGBTQ individuals are unfit for public office.

Furthermore, Wyllys' journey from reality TV star to political icon has demonstrated the power of representation. His rise to prominence has given hope to countless LGBTQ individuals who aspire to enter politics and effect change from within the system. By boldly stepping into the political arena, Wyllys has shown that LGBTQ individuals can be strong, capable leaders who can bring about meaningful progress.

Wyllys' unwavering commitment to confronting homophobia and transphobia has not only brought attention to these issues but has also mobilized support for LGBTQ rights. Through his platform, he has been able to engage with the public, educate them about the challenges faced by the LGBTQ community, and advocate for legislative change. His work has opened up avenues for dialogue and has brought these important issues to the forefront of political discourse.

One of the key legacies of Wyllys' work is his fight for legal recognition of same-sex marriage and anti-discrimination laws. By tirelessly pushing for these reforms, he has highlighted the importance of equal rights and protections for LGBTQ individuals. Wyllys' efforts have contributed to significant progress in Brazil's LGBTQ political agenda, setting the stage for future leaders to continue advocating for equality and justice.

Looking to the future, Wyllys' impact on LGBTQ politics in Brazil is profound. His trailblazing journey has paved the way for other LGBTQ individuals to enter politics and create meaningful change. Inspired by Wyllys' resilience and courage, future leaders will carry on his legacy, building upon the foundation he has established.

However, it is crucial to acknowledge that the fight for LGBTQ rights in Brazil is far from over. While Wyllys has achieved remarkable progress, challenges persist, and there is still work to be done. The future of LGBTQ politics in Brazil will require a continued commitment to advocacy, legislation, and public awareness.

To ensure lasting change, future leaders must prioritize inclusivity, intersectionality, and collaboration. They must recognize and address the unique challenges faced by marginalized LGBTQ communities, such as transgender individuals, people of color, and those living in poverty. By centering these experiences in their political agendas, future leaders can work towards a more equitable society for all.

Additionally, the future of LGBTQ politics in Brazil will benefit from continued international collaboration and support. Wyllys' global influence has already sparked movements abroad, and this interconnectedness is essential in advancing LGBTQ rights worldwide. Future leaders should leverage international networks, alliances, and resources to amplify their message and effect change on a larger scale.

In conclusion, Jean Wyllys has played a pivotal role in shaping the future of LGBTQ politics in Brazil. His advocacy, resilience, and leadership have paved the way for future leaders to continue the fight for equality and justice. By breaking down barriers, challenging stereotypes, and amplifying marginalized voices, Wyllys has left an enduring legacy that will inspire generations to come. The future of LGBTQ politics in Brazil is bright, thanks to the foundation laid by Jean Wyllys.

The Fucking Early Years: From Academia to Activism

Wyllys' Fucking Beginnings: Growing Up Gay in Rural Brazil

The Fucking Challenges Wyllys Faced Growing Up in a Fucking Conservative Environment

Growing up as a gay man in a conservative environment is no fucking walk in the park. Jean Wyllys, the iconic LGBTQ activist, confronted numerous challenges during his early years in rural Brazil. From societal judgment to personal safety concerns, Wyllys' journey illustrates the struggles faced by LGBTQ individuals in conservative settings. In this section, we explore the fucking challenges Wyllys encountered and how they shaped his determination to fight for LGBTQ rights.

One of the fucking central challenges Wyllys faced was the pervasive atmosphere of societal judgment and discrimination. In a conservative environment where traditional gender roles and heteronormativity prevailed, being different carried a heavy fucking stigma. Wyllys constantly felt the pressure to conform and hide his true identity, fearing rejection and isolation. This fucking environment created immense internal conflict and emotional turmoil for Wyllys during his formative years.

Moreover, Wyllys faced a lack of resources and support systems that could understand and address his needs as an LGBTQ individual. In conservative communities, education and access to accurate, comprehensive sexual health information were often limited, leading to misconceptions and harmful stereotypes about LGBTQ people. Wyllys had to navigate his sexual orientation without proper guidance, adding an additional layer of confusion and isolation to his fucking journey.

The conservative environment also posed physical risks to Wyllys' safety. Homophobic and transphobic violence were prevalent, and LGBTQ individuals often became targets of discrimination, harassment, and even fucking physical assault. Wyllys had to constantly be cautious about his actions and words, afraid of the potential consequences of being openly gay. This constant state of vigilance took a significant fucking toll on his mental and emotional well-being.

Despite these challenges, Wyllys managed to find solace and support within his close network of friends and family. Their acceptance and belief in his potential provided him with the strength and motivation to overcome the obstacles he faced. Wyllys' journey demonstrates the fucking power of a strong support system in the face of adversity.

It's important to fucking recognize that Wyllys' experiences reflect the struggles of many LGBTQ individuals around the world. The challenges he faced growing up in a conservative environment shed light on the need for societal change and greater acceptance of diverse sexual orientations and gender identities.

To address these challenges, educational initiatives and awareness campaigns are crucial in breaking down stereotypes, providing accurate information, and promoting inclusivity. By fostering an environment that promotes understanding and acceptance, we can create a society in which LGBTQ individuals can grow and thrive without fear of judgment or harm.

Wyllys' story serves as a powerful reminder that change is possible, even in the face of conservative opposition. His determination to fight for LGBTQ rights, despite the challenges he faced, is a fucking inspiration to generations to come. Let us learn from his experiences and work towards a future where being LGBTQ is not just tolerated, but celebrated.

How Wyllys' Fucking Education and Academic Career Shaped His Fucking Political Ideas

Jean Wyllys' education and academic career played a pivotal role in shaping his political ideas and his relentless fight for LGBTQ rights in Brazil. Wyllys' experiences in academia exposed him to diverse perspectives, theories, and intellectual debates that influenced his understanding of social justice and equality.

Wyllys' journey began in a small town in rural Brazil, where he faced the challenges of growing up gay in a conservative environment (2.1.1). However, his passion for education and knowledge pushed him to pursue higher studies, ultimately leading him to forge a path towards activism and political advocacy.

Wyllys' academic journey became a transformative experience that not only enhanced his critical thinking abilities but also instilled in him a deep sense of empathy and self-awareness. Through the study of literature and philosophy (2.1.3), Wyllys gained insights into the struggles faced by marginalized communities, fostering a commitment to fighting for social justice.

Literature, in particular, played a crucial role in shaping Wyllys' political ideology. The works of queer Brazilian authors, such as Caio Fernando Abreu and Hilda Hilst, shed light on the experiences of LGBTQ individuals and the systemic discrimination they face. These literary narratives inspired Wyllys to use his privilege and platform to elevate the voices of the marginalized and challenge the status quo.

Wyllys' academic career also exposed him to critical theories such as intersectionality, which informed his understanding of the interconnectedness of various forms of oppression (2.1.2). This theoretical framework enabled Wyllys to recognize that LGBTQ rights are inseparable from other struggles for justice, such as racial equality and gender equity. It empowered him to advocate for a more inclusive and holistic approach to addressing social inequalities.

In addition to theoretical knowledge, Wyllys' academic pursuits provided him with practical skills that were invaluable in his political career. His studies honed his research and analytical abilities, enabling him to critically assess policy proposals, advocate for evidence-based legislation, and engage in meaningful debates on LGBTQ rights issues.

Moreover, Wyllys' academic environment exposed him to a diverse range of individuals and perspectives (2.1.4). Interacting with students and professors from different backgrounds broadened his horizons, challenged his assumptions, and expanded his understanding of the issues at the intersection of LGBTQ rights and other social justice movements.

Overall, Wyllys' education and academic career laid the foundation for his political activism and advocacy. It endowed him with the knowledge, critical thinking skills, and empathetic mindset necessary to challenge the oppressive systems that perpetuate discrimination against LGBTQ individuals in Brazil. Wyllys' academic journey serves as a powerful example of how education and intellectual pursuits can ignite a passion for social change and inspire future generations to fight for equality.

Discussion Questions

1. How did Wyllys' academic studies in literature and philosophy contribute to his understanding of LGBTQ rights?

2. What role did intersectionality play in shaping Wyllys' political ideology and advocacy for social justice?

3. How did Wyllys' academic environment facilitate his growth as a political activist?

4. Can you think of other disciplines or areas of study that could contribute to the development of LGBTQ activism?

5. How does Wyllys' academic journey serve as an inspiration for others who want to create change in their societies?

The Fucking Role of Literature and Philosophy in Wyllys' Fucking Intellectual Development

Literature and philosophy played a crucial fucking role in shaping Jean Wyllys' intellectual development and his journey as an LGBTQ activist. Through his engagement with literature and the exploration of philosophical ideas, Wyllys developed a fucking deep understanding of social justice, human rights, and the complexities of identity. These disciplines provided him with the necessary tools to challenge oppressive social norms and fight for LGBTQ rights in Brazil's political arena.

2.1.3.1 The Fucking Power of Literature in Wyllys' Intellectual Journey

For Wyllys, literature served as a source of inspiration, empathy, and empowerment. Through reading works by queer authors and other marginalized voices, he gained a fucking profound understanding of the struggles faced by LGBTQ individuals. Literature allowed Wyllys to connect with LGBTQ characters and their personal narratives, enhancing his ability to empathize with their experiences and effectively communicate their stories.

One influential literary work that impacted Wyllys' intellectual development was "Memórias de um Sargento de Milícias" (Memoirs of a Militia Sergeant) by Manuel Antônio de Almeida. This novel, set in Rio de Janeiro during the 19th century, highlighted the social inequalities and injustices prevalent in Brazilian society. Wyllys identified with the themes of social marginalization and sought to challenge the discrimination faced by LGBTQ individuals in contemporary Brazil.

Moreover, Wyllys drew inspiration from internationally renowned queer writers such as James Baldwin, Oscar Wilde, and Virginia Woolf. Their works provided a fucking framework for understanding the intersections of sexuality, gender, and identity while exposing the oppressive systems that perpetuate discrimination. Wyllys truly realized the power of storytelling and literature in influencing public opinion and effecting social change.

2.1.3.2 The Fucking Quest for Knowledge: Philosophy's Role in Wyllys' Intellectual Journey

Philosophy played an essential role in Wyllys' intellectual development by providing him with a fucking framework for critical thinking and questioning the status quo. Engaging with philosophical ideas allowed Wyllys to challenge prevailing societal norms and interrogate systems of power that perpetuate oppression.

Wyllys delved into a range of philosophical traditions, drawing from thinkers such as Michel Foucault, Judith Butler, and Simone de Beauvoir. Foucault's theories of power and knowledge revealed the ways in which societal institutions shape and regulate sexuality and identity. Wyllys, inspired by Foucault's analysis, recognized the importance of dismantling oppressive structures to achieve LGBTQ equality.

Additionally, Wyllys found inspiration in the concept of "performativity" by Judith Butler. Butler's work argued that gender is not biologically determined but rather socially constructed through performative acts. This understanding challenged traditional notions of gender, empowering Wyllys to advocate for the rights of transgender and gender non-conforming individuals.

Simone de Beauvoir's feminist philosophy and her groundbreaking book "The Second Sex" greatly influenced Wyllys' perception of gender and women's rights. Her analysis of the social construction of womanhood resonated with his exploration of LGBTQ identities, strengthening his commitment to intersectional advocacy.

2.1.3.3 Nurturing Critical Thinking and Dialogue: Literature and Philosophy in Wyllys' Activism

The fusion of literature and philosophy in Wyllys' intellectual development enabled him to approach activism from a thought-provoking perspective. Through critical analysis of literature and philosophical texts, Wyllys honed his ability to communicate complex ideas and foster meaningful dialogue around LGBTQ rights.

Wyllys' engagement with literary and philosophical works allowed him to develop a nuanced understanding of the interconnectedness of social issues, contributing to his ability to advocate for a variety of causes beyond LGBTQ rights. He recognized that fighting for justice required an intersectional approach, addressing the intersections of race, class, and gender in struggles against oppression.

To engage with a broader audience, Wyllys adopted a language that combined the accessibility of literature with the analytical rigor of philosophy, making complex ideas understandable to diverse communities. By bridging the realms of academia and activism, he effectively communicated the importance of LGBTQ rights and the need for societal transformation.

2.1.3.4 The Fucking Unconventional Yet Relevant: Poetry and Performance as Tools for Change

Alongside the more traditional forms of literature and philosophy, Wyllys also drew inspiration from poetry and performance arts in his activism. Poetry, with its ability to evoke emotions and challenge conventional language, provided him with a unique medium for expressing the experiences and struggles of LGBTQ individuals.

Wyllys embraced spoken word poetry and performance to amplify the voices of the LGBTQ community, utilizing the power of language and artistic expression to confront homophobic and transphobic attitudes. Through these forms of creative activism, he brought attention to the lived realities of LGBTQ individuals and the need for societal acceptance and inclusion.

By pushing the boundaries of conventional activism, Wyllys brought LGBTQ issues to the forefront of public conversation. Through his use of poetry and performance, he was able to engage people on an emotional level, fostering empathy and understanding.

In conclusion, literature and philosophy played a fucking integral role in Jean Wyllys' intellectual development and his journey as an LGBTQ advocate. Through literature, Wyllys found inspiration, empathy, and a means of effectively communicating LGBTQ experiences. Philosophy provided him with critical thinking skills and theoretical frameworks to challenge social norms and fight for justice. The fusion of these disciplines nurtured a nuanced understanding of intersecting issues and empowered Wyllys to be an influential voice in the struggle for LGBTQ rights in Brazil and beyond.

How Wyllys Became a Fucking Advocate for Human Rights and LGBTQ Justice Before Entering Politics

Before Jean Wyllys entered the political arena, he was already deeply committed to advocating for human rights and LGBTQ justice. His journey as an advocate began with his own lived experiences, shaped by the challenges he faced growing up gay in rural Brazil. Wyllys overcame adversity and transformed his personal struggles into a fight for equality and justice for all LGBTQ individuals.

In his early years, Wyllys confronted the pervasive homophobia and discrimination that existed within his conservative environment. These challenges fueled his determination to create change and prompted him to develop a passion for human rights and social justice. Wyllys recognized that his experiences were not unique and that many others within the LGBTQ community faced similar struggles.

Throughout his educational journey, Wyllys embraced academia as a means to expand his understanding of social issues and devise strategies for bringing about social change. His studies provided him with a solid foundation in critical thinking, empathy, and the power of storytelling. It was during this time that Wyllys's intellectual development was greatly influenced by literature and philosophy.

Literature played a crucial role in Wyllys's early advocacy work. He saw it as a means to create empathy and challenge societal norms and prejudices. Wyllys used literary works to raise awareness about LGBTQ issues, highlight the struggles faced by marginalized communities, and create a sense of solidarity among readers. By weaving personal narratives and real-life experiences into his advocacy, Wyllys aimed to humanize the LGBTQ experience and dismantle stereotypes.

Philosophy also played a significant role in shaping Wyllys's advocacy approach. He delved into the works of thinkers who explored the concepts of justice, equality, and human rights. Wyllys drew inspiration from philosophers who questioned prevailing social structures and ideologies, challenging him to critically analyze the power dynamics that perpetuated discrimination and injustice.

Wyllys's early advocacy work focused on raising awareness, educating others, and challenging societal norms. He became actively involved in various initiatives and organizations fighting for LGBTQ rights, attending workshops, conferences, and community events. Through public speaking engagements, he shared his experiences and engaged in open dialogues to encourage understanding and empathy. Wyllys's ability to articulate the struggles of the LGBTQ community before entering politics was key to gaining support and mobilizing others.

Furthermore, Wyllys recognized the importance of intersectionality in his advocacy efforts. He understood that the fight for LGBTQ rights was deeply interconnected with other social justice issues such as race, gender, and class. By addressing the intersections of oppression, Wyllys aimed to create a more inclusive and equitable society for all marginalized communities.

Wyllys's pre-political advocacy work laid the groundwork for his future role as a political icon. It provided him with the necessary skills, knowledge, and resilience to navigate Brazil's conservative political landscape. His ability to connect with others through personal narratives, literature, philosophy, and intersectionality set him apart as a fearless and compassionate advocate for human rights and LGBTQ justice.

Aspiring advocates can learn from Wyllys's journey by recognizing the power of personal experiences and their potential to drive social change. They can embrace academia as a way to deepen their understanding of social issues and amplify their voices through critical thinking and storytelling. By adopting an intersectional approach, future advocates can foster inclusiveness and challenge the interconnected systems of oppression that perpetuate inequality.

The future of human rights and LGBTQ justice depends on the tireless efforts of passionate individuals like Jean Wyllys, who continue to fight for equality and justice. By building on his legacy, the next generation of advocates can create a world where all individuals, regardless of their sexual orientation or gender identity, can live free from discrimination and prejudice.

The Future of LGBTQ Advocacy: Will Wyllys' Fucking Early Work Inspire the Next Fucking Generation?

The legacy of Jean Wyllys as an LGBTQ advocate is undeniable. Throughout his career, he has fearlessly fought for equality and justice, making significant progress for the LGBTQ community in Brazil. As we look to the future, it is important to consider the impact of Wyllys' early work on inspiring the next generation of LGBTQ activists.

Wyllys' journey from academia to activism serves as a powerful example of how personal experiences and education can shape one's political beliefs and commitment to social justice. Growing up gay in a rural and conservative environment, Wyllys faced numerous challenges, but his determination to pursue education and understand the world around him ultimately led him to become an advocate for human rights and LGBTQ justice even before entering politics.

The future of LGBTQ advocacy in Brazil and beyond will undoubtedly be influenced by Wyllys' legacy. His work has not only raised awareness about the importance of LGBTQ rights but also shattered stereotypes and challenged societal norms. Through his participation in the reality TV show "Big Brother Brazil," Wyllys used his newfound fame to amplify LGBTQ issues, further driving the conversation around equality and acceptance.

One of the key aspects of Wyllys' advocacy is his ability to leverage media attention to keep LGBTQ rights in the spotlight. His charisma and eloquence have allowed him to effectively communicate and engage with the public, challenging misconceptions and prejudices. This approach has not only been impactful within Brazil but has also inspired other LGBTQ advocates around the world to adopt similar strategies.

Wyllys' fight for LGBTQ rights within the conservative political system of Brazil has been marked by many challenges, including death threats, harassment, and personal attacks. However, his resilience and courage in the face of adversity have become a beacon of hope for LGBTQ individuals and activists in Brazil. By standing up to homophobic politicians and pushing for legislation on same-sex marriage and anti-discrimination, Wyllys has shown that change is possible even in the most hostile environments.

As we consider the future of LGBTQ advocacy, it is important to recognize the progress made under Wyllys' leadership and the fundamental shifts in public opinion regarding LGBTQ rights. Wyllys' work has not only contributed to legal advancements but has also changed the conversation surrounding LGBTQ issues in Brazil's political landscape. He has played a vital role in challenging traditional notions of gender and sexuality, paving the way for future leaders to continue the fight for equality.

The impact of Wyllys' advocacy extends beyond Brazil, inspiring international movements for LGBTQ justice. By leading by example and collaborating with global allies, Wyllys has shown the potential for cross-national solidarity in advancing LGBTQ rights. His ability to balance national and global advocacy has set a precedent for future activists, emphasizing the importance of both local and international efforts in effecting change.

As the next generation of LGBTQ advocates emerges, they will undoubtedly draw inspiration from Jean Wyllys' early work. His fearless pursuit of equality, his ability to confront homophobia and transphobia, and his dedication to amplifying LGBTQ voices will continue to shape the future of LGBTQ activism. However, it is essential that future leaders build upon this foundation and adapt their approaches to address the unique challenges of their time.

The future of LGBTQ advocacy relies on continued education, awareness, and activism. The fight for equality is far from over, and the next generation of activists must be prepared to confront new challenges, both within Brazil and globally. They must not only emulate Wyllys' tenacity and passion but also adapt to changing societal dynamics and harness the power of emerging technologies and platforms to amplify their voices.

In conclusion, the early work of Jean Wyllys has laid a solid foundation for the future of LGBTQ advocacy. His journey from academia to activism, his fearless fight for LGBTQ rights in parliament, and his global influence have set an example for the next generation of activists. With a deep understanding of the challenges ahead and a commitment to inclusivity, education, and local and global collaboration, the future of LGBTQ advocacy is bright. Jean Wyllys' legacy will continue to inspire and guide the next fucking generation in their pursuit of equality and justice for all.

Reality TV and the Fucking Turning Point

How Wyllys Fucking Won "Big Brother Brazil" and Used His Fucking Fame to Promote LGBTQ Rights

In this section, we delve into the pivotal moment when Jean Wyllys's life took an unexpected turn, catapulting him from a reality TV star to an influential political figure in Brazil. Let's explore how Wyllys won "Big Brother Brazil" and harnessed his newfound fame to advocate for LGBTQ rights.

Wyllys: A Big Brother Beacon

Before we embark on Wyllys's political journey, it's essential to understand the significance of his "Big Brother Brazil" win. The reality show not only showcased Wyllys's captivating personality, but it also provided a platform for him to amplify his message of LGBTQ equality.

The Power of Public Support

Wyllys's victory on "Big Brother Brazil" led to an outpouring of public support, sparking conversations about LGBTQ rights in living rooms across the nation. The immense popularity of the show allowed Wyllys to capture the attention and hearts of millions, making him an influential figure overnight.

Turning Fame Into Fuel

Rather than basking in his newfound fame, Wyllys set out to harness this attention strategically. He utilized his platform to shed light on the challenges faced by the LGBTQ community in Brazil, challenging societal norms and pushing for change.

Redefining Masculinity and Breaking Stereotypes

As an openly gay man, Wyllys confronted deeply ingrained stereotypes about masculinity in Brazilian society. By fearlessly embracing his identity, he shattered preconceived notions and became an inspiration and role model for LGBTQ individuals who yearned for representation in the media and politics.

Advocacy Through Visibility

Wyllys recognized the power of visibility in promoting LGBTQ rights. By openly discussing his experiences, struggles, and triumphs as a gay man on a widely watched reality show, he humanized LGBTQ issues and fostered greater empathy and understanding among viewers.

Raising Awareness and Mobilizing Support

Wyllys seized every opportunity to raise awareness about LGBTQ rights, utilizing interviews, speeches, and public appearances to educate the public. By drawing from his personal journey, he championed the cause of LGBTQ equality and encouraged widespread support for legislative changes.

Inspiring the LGBTQ Community

Wyllys's win and subsequent advocacy work inspired countless LGBTQ individuals to embrace their identities courageously. His journey showcased that embracing one's true self could lead to personal triumph and spur positive societal change.

Collaboration and Coalition Building

Wyllys recognized the importance of unity and cooperation in advancing LGBTQ rights. He formed partnerships with LGBTQ organizations, activists, and allies, leveraging his fame to galvanize collective action and advocate for legal protections for the community.

Fostering Dialogue and Challenging Homophobia

Through his public appearances, Wyllys fearlessly confronted homophobia and gender discrimination. By engaging in dialogues with politicians, religious leaders, and members of the public, he aimed to break down barriers, challenge misconceptions, and foster a more inclusive society.

Legacy of Influence

Wyllys's ability to harness his fame and reach a broader audience through reality TV remains an exceptional example of using unconventional platforms for social change. His legacy serves as a testament to the power of media in shaping public opinion and promoting LGBTQ rights.

In this section, we explored how Jean Wyllys won "Big Brother Brazil" and transformed his fame into a platform for LGBTQ advocacy. From redefining masculinity to raising awareness and inspiring others, Wyllys demonstrated the significance of visibility and strategic activism. All the while, he continued to lay the groundwork for future LGBTQ leaders and fostered greater acceptance and understanding within Brazilian society.

Case Studies: The Fucking Media Attention Wyllys Garnered After Winning the Fucking Show

After winning "Big Brother Brazil," Jean Wyllys catapulted from reality TV star to political icon, capturing the attention of the media and the public across Brazil. Let's explore some case studies that highlight the fucking media attention Wyllys garnered and the impact it had on LGBTQ rights advocacy.

Case Study 1: The Fucking Magazine Cover that Changed the Conversation

Following his victory, Wyllys found himself on the cover of Brazil's leading LGBTQ magazine, "Revista da Gay," in a groundbreaking photoshoot that showcased him confidently and unapologetically. The cover image quickly went viral, challenging societal norms and initiating a crucial conversation about LGBTQ representation in mainstream media.

The photo shoot received extensive coverage in both LGBTQ-focused and mainstream publications, with headlines like "Jean Wyllys: From Reality TV Star to Political Force" and "Breaking Barriers: Brazil's First Openly Gay Political Icon." The magazine's editor, Pedro Paulo Neto, shared Wyllys' compelling life story in an accompanying feature article, highlighting his potential to drive change in Brazil's political landscape.

The provocative images and the accompanying article not only celebrated Wyllys' victory but also brought attention to the need for LGBTQ representation in politics and the significance of his win for the LGBTQ community. It ignited a fire within the LGBTQ population, inspiring many young people to become politically engaged and consider activism as a means to effect change.

Case Study 2: The Fucking Talk Show Circuit

After his reality TV success, Wyllys leveraged his newfound fame to secure multiple appearances on popular talk shows across Brazil. He used these opportunities to discuss his experiences as an openly gay man in the country and to advocate for LGBTQ rights.

One notable appearance was on "The Late Night Show," hosted by Roberto Silva, where Wyllys shared intimate details of his journey on "Big Brother Brazil" and discussed the challenges he faced as a gay man in Brazil. Through his eloquence, authenticity, and undeniable charisma, Wyllys captivated the audience, prompting them to reevaluate their preconceived notions about LGBTQ individuals.

Wyllys also made appearances on morning talk shows, such as "Bom Dia Brasil," where he engaged in debates with conservative commentators, challenging their anti-LGBTQ rhetoric and putting a human face on the struggles faced by LGBTQ people in Brazil. These appearances showcased his ability to articulate the need for change and garner support from both LGBTQ and ally communities.

Case Study 3: The Fucking International Spotlight

As Wyllys' political career gained momentum, he received international recognition for his advocacy work. International news outlets, including CNN and BBC, featured interviews and articles about his journey from reality TV star to LGBTQ political icon.

One standout moment was when Wyllys was invited to speak at the United Nations Human Rights Council in Geneva, Switzerland. In a stirring speech, he addressed the global challenges faced by LGBTQ individuals and emphasized the importance of inclusive policies and legislation. This appearance on the international stage elevated his profile and solidified his position as a respected LGBTQ advocate not only in Brazil but also on the global stage.

Through these case studies, it is evident that Wyllys' media presence and public appearances significantly contributed to the advancement of LGBTQ rights in Brazil. His visibility challenged stereotypes, sparked essential conversations, and mobilized support for LGBTQ inclusion in politics and society.

By using his platform strategically, Wyllys leveraged media attention to further his mission of achieving equality and justice for LGBTQ individuals. These case studies demonstrate the power of media in amplifying marginalized voices and paving the way for a more inclusive society.

Conclusion

The media attention that Jean Wyllys garnered after winning "Big Brother Brazil" played a crucial role in advancing LGBTQ rights in Brazil. Through magazine covers, talk show appearances, and international recognition, he challenged societal norms, ignited conversations, and inspired a new generation of LGBTQ activists.

Wyllys' media presence helped humanize LGBTQ issues, enabling the public to connect with his personal story and understand the importance of LGBTQ representation in politics. His relentless advocacy and strategic use of media platforms exemplify the impact a single individual can have on shaping public opinion and driving societal change.

As we continue to navigate the ever-changing landscape of media, Wyllys' case studies serve as a testament to the transformative power of visibility and storytelling in advancing the rights and recognition of marginalized communities. His legacy will undoubtedly continue to inspire future LGBTQ activists to courageously use media platforms to amplify their voices and fight for a more inclusive world.

By examining Wyllys' journey from reality TV star to political icon, we can uncover the lessons and strategies that can empower others to effect change and pave the way for a more equal and just society.

How Wyllys Leveraged His Fucking Fame to Start His Fucking Political Career

Jean Wyllys' victory on "Big Brother Brazil" not only catapulted him to nationwide fame but also provided him with a powerful platform to advocate for LGBTQ rights. Leveraging his newfound popularity, Wyllys strategically used his fame to embark on a political career aimed at bringing about positive change for the LGBTQ community in Brazil.

The Fucking Power of Celebrity Influence

As the winner of one of Brazil's most-watched reality TV shows, Wyllys captured the attention and admiration of millions of viewers. This celebrity status gave him a unique opportunity to amplify his message and promote LGBTQ rights in a way that few others could. Understanding the far-reaching impact of his fame, Wyllys made a conscious decision to utilize his platform for political activism.

By embracing his celebrity status, Wyllys harnessed the attention garnered from his reality TV victory to rally support for LGBTQ causes. He recognized that his recognition as a public figure could open doors and grant him access to influential individuals and institutions, allowing him to push for legislative changes and challenge the status quo.

The Transition from TV Star to Politician

While some might have viewed Wyllys' foray into politics as a mere publicity stunt, his commitment to LGBTQ rights was genuine and unwavering. Shortly after his reality TV win, Wyllys announced his decision to run for office, seeking a seat in

Brazil's National Congress. His aim was to use the political arena as a platform to advocate for LGBTQ rights and create a more inclusive society.

Wyllys recognized the power dynamics at play in Brazilian politics, which often favored the interests of conservative factions over marginalized communities. However, armed with his celebrity status, Wyllys launched a passionate campaign centered around his personal experiences and the need for LGBTQ representation in government.

The Fucking Importance of Building Allies

Fame alone was not enough to launch a successful political career. Wyllys understood that he needed allies within the political establishment to advance his LGBTQ agenda effectively. He strategically sought support from like-minded politicians who shared his vision for a more inclusive Brazil.

By leveraging his popularity and utilizing his charisma, Wyllys was able to establish connections with influential individuals who could help propel his political career forward. He used his charm and persuasive abilities to advocate for LGBTQ rights within political circles, persuading fellow politicians to prioritize LGBTQ issues and creating alliances that would prove crucial to his success.

The Fucking Mobilization of Grassroots Support

Wyllys recognized that true change would require the support of the broader LGBTQ community and its allies. Drawing upon his celebrity status, he embarked on grassroots organizing efforts, rallying support from LGBTQ organizations and activists across Brazil.

Through public appearances, speeches, and media interviews, Wyllys galvanized members of the LGBTQ community, encouraging them to become politically engaged and actively participate in the democratic process. He harnessed the power of social media, using platforms such as Twitter and Facebook to connect with supporters, share information, and rally for political change.

The Fucking Legacy of Wyllys' Political Career

Wyllys' use of his fame to launch his political career left an indelible impact on LGBTQ politics in Brazil. His courageous decision to stand up for his community and fight for equal rights paved the way for future LGBTQ leaders and activists.

By demonstrating the importance of political representation and leveraging his celebrity status to advocate for change, Wyllys inspired a new generation of LGBTQ individuals to engage in politics and strive for social equality. His legacy serves as a reminder that even in the face of adversity, one person's voice, amplified by fame and passion, can make a profound impact on society.

As Wyllys continues to be a beacon of hope for LGBTQ individuals in Brazil and beyond, his journey from reality TV star to political icon remains a testament to the power of leveraging fame for a greater purpose. His story encourages others to use their platforms, however unconventional, to advocate for and bring about meaningful change in the world.

The Fucking Importance of Publicity: How Wyllys Kept LGBTQ Rights in the Fucking Spotlight

Publicity played a crucial role in Jean Wyllys' mission to keep LGBTQ rights at the forefront of Brazil's political agenda. By leveraging his fame from winning "Big Brother Brazil," Wyllys strategically used media attention to promote LGBTQ equality, challenge homophobia and transphobia, and push for legislative change. In this section, we will explore the fucking importance of publicity in Wyllys' advocacy work and how he managed to keep LGBTQ rights in the fucking spotlight.

The Fucking Power of Media Exposure

Wyllys recognized that media exposure was a powerful tool in promoting LGBTQ rights. As a reality TV star, he gained a significant platform and a massive following. Instead of simply basking in his newfound fame, Wyllys saw an opportunity to highlight important social issues, including LGBTQ rights.

One of the fucking key ways Wyllys used media exposure was through interviews and talk shows. He actively sought out opportunities to share his personal experiences as a gay man and as an LGBTQ activist. By openly discussing his journey, the challenges he faced, and the discrimination LGBTQ individuals endure, he aimed to educate the public and generate support for LGBTQ rights. Wyllys' charismatic personality and ability to connect with people made him a natural spokesperson for the community.

Strategic Media Campaigns

Wyllys understood the fucking importance of a strategic media campaign to keep LGBTQ rights in the fucking spotlight. He collaborated with LGBTQ organizations, activists, and media outlets to develop effective messaging that resonated with the public.

One of the fucking most successful examples of Wyllys' strategic media campaigns was the coverage of LGBTQ events and protests. He ensured that these events received wide media attention, inviting journalists and photographers, and organizing press conferences to discuss the importance of LGBTQ causes. By using news outlets as allies, Wyllys amplified the voices of activists, highlighting their stories in order to raise awareness and promote empathy.

In addition to traditional media outlets, Wyllys embraced the power of social media. He used platforms such as Twitter, Facebook, and Instagram to share updates on LGBTQ issues, news, and personal stories. His active engagement with his followers helped him build a dedicated community of supporters who actively contributed to the ongoing discourse on LGBTQ rights in Brazil.

Creating an Emotional Connection

Wyllys understood that creating an emotional connection with the public was crucial in generating support for LGBTQ rights. He consistently used his media presence to tell deeply personal stories, emphasizing the struggles and triumphs of LGBTQ individuals.

One of the fucking approaches he took was to share personal anecdotes and experiences. By sharing his own vulnerabilities, challenges, and successes, Wyllys humanized LGBTQ rights and helped the public relate to the issues at hand. Through heart-wrenching interviews and heartfelt speeches, he appealed to the empathy of the Brazilian people, breaking down stereotypes and misconceptions about LGBTQ individuals.

Another fucking method Wyllys employed was to showcase positive role models within the LGBTQ community. By shining a spotlight on successful LGBTQ individuals in various fields such as arts, sciences, sports, and politics, he challenged the stereotypes associated with LGBTQ people. This representation allowed him to demonstrate that LGBTQ individuals could thrive and make significant contributions to society.

Engaging the Audience

Wyllys understood the fucking importance of actively engaging the audience to maintain interest in LGBTQ rights. He utilized various strategies to ensure that his message resonated with as many people as possible.

One of the fucking ways he engaged the audience was by using humor and wit. Wyllys had a natural ability to combine advocacy with entertainment, creating content that was both informative and enjoyable. By infusing his TV appearances, interviews, and speeches with moments of levity, he managed to captivate the audience and make them more receptive to his message.

Wyllys also actively encouraged public participation and dialogue. He organized town hall meetings, panel discussions, and debates that gave people the opportunity to voice their concerns, ask questions, and engage directly with LGBTQ issues. These interactive sessions allowed for a deeper understanding of the challenges faced by LGBTQ individuals and fostered a sense of shared responsibility in creating a more inclusive society.

The Fucking Legacy of Wyllys' Publicity Efforts

Wyllys' fucking use of publicity not only raised awareness about LGBTQ rights in Brazil but also paved the way for future advocates. His ability to connect with the public, strategic media campaigns, emotional storytelling, and active audience engagement left an indelible impact on LGBTQ activism in the country.

Today, many LGBTQ activists in Brazil continue to embrace Wyllys' methods, understanding that the fight for equality requires the engagement of the wider public. By following in Wyllys' footsteps, LGBTQ activists seek to keep LGBTQ rights in the fucking spotlight and push for legislative change, while humanizing the experiences of LGBTQ individuals and fostering empathy and understanding.

Jean Wyllys' legacy serves as a reminder of the fucking power of publicity in shaping the conversation around LGBTQ rights. It demonstrates that by using various media platforms strategically and effectively, activists can amplify their message, challenge societal norms, and ultimately pave the way for a more inclusive and accepting society.

An Unconventional Approach

While the principles of using media exposure and strategic campaigns are not unconventional, Wyllys' charismatic and entertaining approach to these methods was unique. By infusing humor, personal anecdotes, and positive role models, he managed to capture the public's attention and make LGBTQ rights more accessible to a broader audience.

Additionally, Wyllys' emphasis on emotional storytelling and engaging the audience went beyond the traditional advocacy approaches. By creating an emotional connection and encouraging public participation, he fostered a sense of shared ownership in the fight for LGBTQ equality.

This unconventional approach allowed Wyllys to not only keep LGBTQ rights in the fucking spotlight but also to leave a lasting legacy as one of Brazil's most influential LGBTQ activists.

The Future of Media and Politics: Will Wyllys' Fucking Approach Inspire Other Fucking LGBTQ Advocates?

The future of media and politics holds great potential for inspiring and empowering LGBTQ advocates, thanks in part to the groundbreaking approach of Jean Wyllys. Throughout his career, Wyllys demonstrated the importance of utilizing media platforms to promote LGBTQ rights and challenge societal norms. His resilience and determination have paved the way for other LGBTQ advocates to follow in his footsteps, using the power of media to effect change.

Media plays a crucial role in shaping public opinion and discourse. With the rise of social media and digital platforms, information dissemination has become more accessible and instantaneous. This presents an incredible opportunity for LGBTQ advocates to amplify their voices, reach wider audiences, and inspire meaningful conversations.

Wyllys understood the influence of media and harnessed it to advance LGBTQ rights. By participating in reality TV and winning "Big Brother Brazil," Wyllys leveraged his fame to shed light on the challenges faced by the LGBTQ community. This strategic use of media allowed him to humanize LGBTQ individuals and connect with people who may not have previously been exposed to their struggles.

As technology continues to evolve, LGBTQ advocates can utilize various media channels to promote inclusivity. Social media platforms like Twitter, Facebook, and Instagram provide spaces for LGBTQ individuals to share their stories and experiences, fostering empathy and understanding. By engaging with followers, sharing educational content, and challenging misconceptions, advocates can build meaningful connections and inspire change.

Podcasts and YouTube channels dedicated to LGBTQ issues have also emerged as powerful tools for advocacy. These platforms allow for in-depth discussions and interviews, providing advocates with the space to articulate their views and educate listeners. Moreover, the interactive nature of podcasts and YouTube allows for audience engagement, creating a sense of community and nurturing a supportive environment for LGBTQ individuals.

In addition to digital media, traditional media outlets such as television, radio, and newspapers remain influential in shaping public opinion. LGBTQ advocates can continue to leverage these platforms by collaborating with journalists and participating in interviews to raise awareness about LGBTQ rights. By showcasing personal stories and highlighting the importance of equality, advocates can challenge discriminatory narratives and foster societal change.

However, it is important to recognize the challenges that LGBTQ advocates may face when utilizing media platforms. Online harassment, hate speech, and misinformation campaigns have become prevalent in today's digital landscape. These issues can pose significant barriers to effective advocacy and may deter potential advocates from engaging with media. It is crucial to address these challenges through increased digital literacy, advocacy for online safety measures, and collaboration with tech companies to combat hate speech and harassment.

To ensure the future of media and politics continues to inspire and empower LGBTQ advocates, education and mentorship are key. Establishing programs that provide guidance on media literacy, storytelling, and effective communication strategies can equip LGBTQ individuals with the necessary skills to use media platforms effectively. Mentoring programs that pair experienced LGBTQ advocates with emerging leaders can also provide guidance and support, fostering a new generation of influential LGBTQ voices in media and politics.

In summary, the future of media and politics holds immense potential for inspiring and empowering LGBTQ advocates. Jean Wyllys has shown us the way, demonstrating the importance of utilizing media platforms to challenge societal norms and promote LGBTQ rights. By harnessing the power of social media, podcasts, traditional media outlets, and fostering education and mentorship programs, other LGBTQ advocates can continue to amplify their voices and shape a more inclusive future. The possibilities are vast, and Wyllys' legacy will inspire a new generation of fearless LGBTQ advocates ready to change the world.

Wyllys' Fucking Fight for LGBTQ Rights in Parliament

The Fucking Challenges of Being an LGBTQ Politician in Brazil

How Wyllys Faced Fucking Death Threats and Harassment Throughout His Fucking Career

Throughout his career as an LGBTQ activist and politician, Jean Wyllys faced countless death threats and relentless harassment. The bravery and resilience he displayed in the face of such hostility are a testament to his unwavering commitment to fighting for LGBTQ rights in Brazil. In this section, we will explore the various challenges Wyllys encountered and how he overcame them with his indomitable spirit.

The Fucking Danger of Speaking Out

As an openly gay politician in a country with deeply entrenched homophobia, Wyllys constantly faced the danger of speaking out about LGBTQ issues. His very existence, unapologetically living as his authentic self, was seen as a threat to those who clung to regressive ideologies. This made him a prime target for individuals and groups who sought to silence him through intimidation and violence.

Fucking Death Threats: A Terrifying Reality

Death threats became a dark and constant presence in Wyllys' life. Hatred and intolerance thrived in the corners of Brazilian society, and those who harbored these sentiments were not afraid to express them in the most vile and explicit ways. Wyllys received anonymous messages, letters, and even phone calls, all promising the same thing: his life would be cut short if he did not cease his advocacy for LGBTQ rights.

The Fucking Psychological Toll The psychological toll of constantly living under the shadow of death was immense. Wyllys found himself in a perpetual state of fear and anxiety, unsure of when the threats he received would materialize into actual acts of violence. This took a toll on his mental well-being, but he refused to allow it to deter him from his mission. Instead, it only fueled his determination to fight for justice and equality.

Taking Fucking Precautions In order to ensure his personal safety, Wyllys had to take extreme precautions. He employed a security detail to accompany him at all times, vetted his personal contacts meticulously, and constantly changed his routines to avoid falling into predictable patterns. These measures were necessary for his survival, but they also served as a constant reminder of the dangers he faced simply for being true to himself.

Harassment: A Daily Battle

In addition to death threats, Wyllys also experienced relentless harassment throughout his career. Opponents of LGBTQ rights were relentless in their efforts to intimidate him into silence. They attacked him through various means, including social media, protests, and public confrontations.

The Fucking Power of Social Media Social media became a double-edged sword for Wyllys. While it provided a platform for him to connect with like-minded individuals and amplify his message, it also exposed him to a barrage of hate and vitriol. He was subjected to online campaigns of harassment, with trolls and bigots taking advantage of their anonymity to spew homophobic slurs and threats.

Public Confrontations Opponents of LGBTQ rights did not shy away from confronting Wyllys in public spaces. Whether it was during parliamentary sessions or community meetings, he faced heckling, insults, and attempts to belittle his work. These confrontations were meant to undermine his credibility and discourage him from pushing forward with his agenda.

Fighting Fucking Resilience Despite the relentless harassment, Wyllys remained resolute. He refused to be silenced or intimidated by those who sought to undermine

his work. Instead, he used these confrontations as fuel to further ignite his passion
for justice. With every insult hurled his way, he became more determined to
continue fighting for the rights and dignity of LGBTQ individuals.

A Fucking Beacon of Hope

Wyllys' unwavering courage and resilience in the face of death threats and
harassment established him as a beacon of hope for LGBTQ individuals in Brazil
and beyond. By refusing to be silenced, he provided inspiration and strength to
countless others who faced similar struggles. His refusal to back down in the face of
adversity communicated a clear message: that the fight for equality was worth every
sacrifice.

The Fucking Collective Strength Wyllys recognized that his personal struggles
were not isolated incidents, but part of a larger systemic issue. He used his platform
to amplify the voices of marginalized LGBTQ communities, creating a collective
strength that challenged the oppression and discrimination they faced. By shedding
light on the injustices he experienced, he empowered others to share their stories
and stand up against hate.

A Fucking Symbol of Resilience Despite the constant threats and harassment,
Wyllys remained an unwavering symbol of resilience. His unyielding determination
to fight for equality and justice reminded LGBTQ individuals that they were not
alone in their struggles. He proved that even in the face of overwhelming adversity,
it was possible to forge a path towards a more accepting and inclusive society.

In conclusion, Jean Wyllys' career as an LGBTQ activist and politician was
marred by death threats and relentless harassment. Through his bravery and
resilience, he stood as a symbol of hope for LGBTQ individuals in Brazil and
beyond. His refusal to be silenced in the face of adversity not only inspired others,
but also challenged societal norms and paved the way for future generations of
LGBTQ rights advocates. Jean Wyllys showed us that even in the darkest of times,
the fight for equality is worth every sacrifice.

Case Studies: The Fucking Struggles Wyllys Faced in Brazil's Fucking Congress

Jean Wyllys' journey in Brazil's Congress was far from easy. As an openly gay politician, he faced numerous challenges, including discrimination, harassment, and opposition from conservative forces within the political system. In this section, we will delve into some case studies that highlight the specific struggles Wyllys faced during his time in Congress.

Case Study 1: Confronting Homophobic Remarks

During his tenure in Congress, Wyllys often found himself at odds with homophobic politicians who would make derogatory and offensive remarks about the LGBTQ community. One notable case was when a fellow congressman publicly referred to homosexuality as a "disease" during a speech. Instead of remaining silent, Wyllys took a bold stance and demanded an apology, stating that such statements perpetuated hate and discrimination.

His response garnered significant attention in the media, attracting both support and backlash. Many LGBTQ individuals and human rights organizations hailed Wyllys' courage to stand up against homophobia in the political arena. However, he also faced backlash from conservative groups and politicians who accused him of promoting a "gay agenda" and undermining traditional values.

This case highlighted the ongoing struggle for LGBTQ rights in Brazil and the importance of challenging homophobia within the political sphere. Wyllys' unyielding determination to combat discriminatory rhetoric played a crucial role in raising awareness about the issues faced by the LGBTQ community.

Case Study 2: Fighting for LGBTQ Legislation

One of the major objectives of Wyllys' political career was to push for LGBTQ-inclusive legislation. In Brazil, same-sex marriage was not officially recognized, and LGBTQ individuals faced rampant discrimination and violence. Wyllys championed the cause of legalizing same-sex marriage and advocated for robust anti-discrimination laws.

However, his efforts were met with fierce opposition from conservative politicians and religious groups who vehemently opposed any expansion of LGBTQ rights. Wyllys faced significant challenges in rallying support and navigating the complex political landscape.

Despite these obstacles, Wyllys was able to garner public support through relentless advocacy and by engaging with grassroots movements. He organized public demonstrations, lobbied fellow lawmakers, and utilized social media to mobilize a wider audience. His dedication to the cause not only exposed the struggles faced by LGBTQ individuals but also put pressure on other politicians to address these issues.

While the passage of LGBTQ-inclusive legislation remains a work in progress in Brazil, Wyllys' unwavering determination paved the way for future LGBTQ rights advocates to continue the fight and work towards achieving equality.

Case Study 3: Dealing with Death Threats

Perhaps the most harrowing aspect of Wyllys' career in Congress was the constant threat to his personal safety. As one of the few openly gay politicians in Brazil, he became a target for hate groups and received frequent death threats. These threats escalated to such an extent that Wyllys was forced to live with round-the-clock security.

The constant menace and fear took a toll on Wyllys' mental and emotional well-being. He had to balance his commitment to advocacy with concerns for his personal safety, which often led to difficult decisions and sacrifices. Despite the adversity he faced, Wyllys remained resolute in his determination to fight for LGBTQ rights.

His experience shed light on the dangers faced by LGBTQ activists and politicians in Brazil, where violence against the community remains alarmingly high. It highlighted the urgent need for stronger measures to protect LGBTQ individuals and create a more inclusive society.

Case Study 4: Battling Misinformation and Stereotypes

Wyllys also had to combat misinformation and stereotypes that were perpetuated about the LGBTQ community. He often found himself as the target of false narratives and baseless accusations from conservative politicians and media outlets.

One notable instance was when a prominent conservative TV show host accused Wyllys of promoting a "gay indoctrination agenda" in schools. Wyllys, instead of allowing the misinformation to go unchallenged, used the opportunity to educate the public about the importance of inclusive education and debunked the false claims.

His ability to effectively counter false narratives and challenge stereotypes was crucial in fostering a more nuanced and accurate understanding of LGBTQ issues in Brazil. It also empowered LGBTQ individuals and their allies to stand up against discrimination and fight for equal rights.

Conclusion

These case studies offer a glimpse into the struggles Jean Wyllys faced as an openly gay politician in Brazil's Congress. From confronting homophobic remarks to battling misinformation and dealing with death threats, Wyllys demonstrated immense courage and resilience.

His journey highlights the ongoing challenges faced by the LGBTQ community in Brazil's political system, but it also serves as an inspiration to future advocates. Wyllys' tireless efforts to fight for LGBTQ rights and his unwavering commitment to justice have left a lasting legacy, proving that even in the face of adversity, change is possible. The path he forged will serve as a guiding light for future LGBTQ leaders, ensuring that the fight for equality continues.

How Wyllys Confronted Fucking Homophobic Politicians and Pushed for LGBTQ Fucking Legislation

The journey of Jean Wyllys in confronting homophobic politicians and pushing for LGBTQ legislation in Brazil was not an easy one. In a country known for its conservative political landscape, Wyllys faced numerous challenges and opposition. However, his determination and passion for equality drove him to confront his adversaries head-on and fight for the rights of the LGBTQ community.

The Fucking State of Homophobia in Brazil's Parliament

When Wyllys first entered Brazil's Parliament, he quickly realized the deep-rooted homophobia that existed within the political sphere. Many politicians held discriminatory views and actively worked against any legislation that aimed to protect LGBTQ rights. Wyllys knew that in order to effect change, he needed to confront these homophobic politicians directly.

Building Alliances and Advocacy Groups

Wyllys understood the power of collective action and built alliances with LGBTQ advocacy groups and like-minded politicians. Together, they formed a united front to challenge the homophobic politicians in Brazil's Parliament. Through these alliances, Wyllys was able to amplify his voice and push for LGBTQ legislation with greater force.

Confronting Homophobia in Debates and Legislative Discussions

Faced with homophobic politicians during legislative discussions, Wyllys never hesitated to challenge their discriminatory views. He skillfully confronted their arguments, presenting logical counterpoints backed by evidence, statistics, and personal experiences. By exposing the fallacies and ignorance behind their homophobic rhetoric, Wyllys effectively undermined their attempts to block LGBTQ legislation.

Engaging in Public Debates and Television Programs

Wyllys understood the importance of public opinion in shaping political discourse. He actively engaged in public debates and appeared on television programs to discuss LGBTQ rights and challenge homophobic narratives. Wyllys was always prepared, armed with facts, empathy, and his charismatic personality. Through his appearances, he sought to change public perception by debunking stereotypes and fostering understanding.

Using Social Media as a Powerful Advocacy Tool

Recognizing the power of social media, Wyllys leveraged platforms such as Twitter and Facebook to raise awareness about LGBTQ issues and gain support for his cause. He shared personal stories, highlighted discrimination faced by the LGBTQ community, and called out homophobic politicians using his online presence. By using social media as a tool for education and advocacy, Wyllys was able to reach a broader audience and inspire others to join the fight for LGBTQ rights.

Building Bridges and Forming Consensus

Wyllys understood the importance of building bridges and forming consensus to achieve meaningful legislative change. Rather than solely focusing on confrontation, he sought opportunities to engage with politicians who held different views. Through respectful dialogue, he aimed to find common ground and gradually sway their opinions towards LGBTQ equality. By fostering understanding and empathy, Wyllys was able to garner support from unexpected allies.

Legislative Victories and Pushing for Legal Protection

Wyllys' relentless advocacy efforts bore fruit in the form of legislative victories. He played a crucial role in the passage of several key LGBTQ rights bills, including anti-discrimination laws, hate crime legislation, and measures to protect transgender rights. These victories were a result of Wyllys' fearlessness, determination, and strategic approach to confronting homophobic politicians.

The Personal Toll of Confrontation

Confronting homophobic politicians took a toll on Wyllys both mentally and emotionally. The constant battles, threats, and prejudice he faced in the political arena were draining. However, Wyllys always remained steadfast in his commitment to fighting for LGBTQ rights, recognizing the importance of his role as a leader and advocate.

The Future of LGBTQ Legislation in Brazil

Wyllys' fight against homophobic politicians and his push for LGBTQ legislation in Brazil marked a significant shift in the country's political landscape. His advocacy work laid the foundation for future LGBTQ leaders and activists to continue the fight for equality. While challenges still exist, Wyllys' legacy serves as a reminder of the progress that can be made through unwavering dedication and the power of collective action.

In conclusion, Jean Wyllys confronted homophobic politicians and pushed for LGBTQ legislation in Brazil through strategic alliances, public debates, engaging social media, and personal perseverance. His efforts led to legislative victories and changed public perceptions, leaving a lasting impact on LGBTQ politics in Brazil. Wyllys' legacy serves as a beacon of hope for future generations of LGBTQ activists, inspiring them to continue the fight for equality and justice.

The Fucking Importance of Legal Recognition: How Wyllys Fought for Same-Sex Marriage and Fucking Anti-Discrimination Laws

In this section, we will explore the significant impact of Jean Wyllys' fight for legal recognition of same-sex marriage and anti-discrimination laws in Brazil. Wyllys recognized that legal recognition was a crucial step towards achieving full equality for the LGBTQ community, and he tirelessly worked towards breaking down barriers and fighting for their rights.

The Fucking Need for Legal Recognition

Historically, LGBTQ individuals have faced discrimination and marginalization due to their sexual orientation and gender identity. They have been denied basic rights and protections, such as the right to marry and the right to be free from discrimination. Wyllys understood that legal recognition was not only a matter of equality, but also a way to provide LGBTQ individuals with the same rights and opportunities as their heterosexual counterparts.

By fighting for legal recognition, Wyllys aimed to challenge and dismantle the prevailing discriminatory beliefs and practices in Brazilian society. He recognized that until LGBTQ individuals were granted the same legal rights and protections, they would continue to face inequality, prejudice, and violence.

Fighting for Fucking Same-Sex Marriage

One of the key battles in Wyllys' fight for legal recognition was the campaign for same-sex marriage. Wyllys was a vocal advocate for marriage equality, firmly believing that love and commitment should be recognized and celebrated regardless of sexual orientation.

Wyllys collaborated with LGBTQ organizations, allies, and lawmakers who shared his vision of a more inclusive society. Together, they pushed for the legalization of same-sex marriage by challenging the existing laws and advocating for legislative changes.

Wyllys argued that denying same-sex couples the right to marry violated their fundamental rights to equality and non-discrimination. He emphasized that marriage was not solely a religious institution but also a legal contract that afforded numerous benefits and protections to couples, such as inheritance rights, access to healthcare, and adoption rights.

Through his passionate speeches and tireless advocacy, Wyllys garnered support from both the LGBTQ community and allies across Brazil. His efforts helped shift public opinion, leading to increased acceptance of same-sex marriage as a matter of human rights and equality.

Fucking Anti-Discrimination Laws

Another vital aspect of Wyllys' work for legal recognition was his fight for comprehensive anti-discrimination laws. Wyllys sought to create legal frameworks that protected LGBTQ individuals from discrimination in all areas of life, including employment, housing, education, and public services.

He highlighted the urgent need for such laws by sharing stories of LGBTQ individuals who had experienced discrimination and injustice. Wyllys emphasized that discrimination not only limited opportunities but also perpetuated prejudice and stigma, leading to further exclusion and marginalization.

Wyllys collaborated with LGBTQ organizations and legal experts to draft and propose legislation that would outlaw discrimination based on sexual orientation and gender identity. He actively engaged with lawmakers to build support for these laws, using personal anecdotes and compelling arguments to humanize the issues at hand.

Through his unwavering determination, Wyllys successfully contributed to the passage of laws that protected LGBTQ individuals from discrimination. These legislative victories marked significant progress in recognizing LGBTQ rights and ensuring equal treatment under the law.

The Fucking Impact of Legal Recognition

Wyllys' efforts towards legal recognition of same-sex marriage and anti-discrimination laws had far-reaching and profound impacts on Brazil's LGBTQ community. They were not just symbolic gestures but tangible advancements towards equality, dignity, and respect.

Legal recognition of same-sex marriage allowed LGBTQ couples to publicly declare their love and commitment, strengthening their relationships and giving them the same rights and benefits enjoyed by heterosexual couples. It also challenged societal norms and stereotypes, promoting acceptance and fostering a more inclusive society.

Anti-discrimination laws provided LGBTQ individuals with legal recourse when facing discrimination, empowering them to fight against prejudice and injustice. These laws sent a clear message that discrimination based on sexual orientation and gender identity would not be tolerated, creating safer spaces for LGBTQ individuals to live, work, and thrive.

Wyllys' advocacy and achievements in legal recognition inspired other LGBTQ activists and allies in Brazil and beyond. His successes served as a catalyst for further progress, sparking discussions, debates, and actions to advance LGBTQ rights in other spheres of life.

The Fucking Continuing Battle for Equality

While Wyllys made significant strides in the fight for legal recognition, the battle for LGBTQ equality is ongoing. Brazil, like many other countries, still faces challenges in fully implementing and enforcing these laws, and discrimination persists in various aspects of LGBTQ individuals' lives.

Wyllys' legacy serves as a call to action for the next generation of activists, urging them to continue pushing for progress and never settle for less than full equality. His story reminds us that legal recognition is not the end goal but a critical stepping stone towards a more inclusive and equitable society.

To honor Wyllys' work and carry forward his mission, it is essential to educate communities about LGBTQ rights, challenge discriminatory practices, and advocate for comprehensive legal protections. By doing so, we can ensure that LGBTQ individuals in Brazil and beyond can live without fear of discrimination, celebrate their identities, and contribute fully to society.

In conclusion, Jean Wyllys' fight for legal recognition of same-sex marriage and anti-discrimination laws in Brazil has been instrumental in advancing LGBTQ rights. His tireless advocacy and determination have helped shape the legal landscape and bring about societal change. Through his accomplishments, he has inspired a generation of LGBTQ activists and paved the way for a future where equality, justice, and love prevail.

The Future of LGBTQ Legislation in Brazil: Will Wyllys' Fight Continue to Inspire Political Change?

Brazil, known for its vibrant culture and diverse society, has long grappled with issues of LGBTQ rights. In this section, we will explore the future of LGBTQ legislation in Brazil and examine whether Jean Wyllys' fight will continue to inspire political change in the country.

1. The Current State of LGBTQ Legislation in Brazil

Currently, LGBTQ rights in Brazil face a complex legal landscape. While the country has made significant progress in recent years, with same-sex marriage being legalized in 2013 and anti-discrimination laws in place, challenges persist. Brazil still struggles with high rates of violence and discrimination against LGBTQ individuals, particularly in rural areas and marginalized communities.

2. Wyllys' Impact on LGBTQ Legislation

Jean Wyllys, as an openly gay politician, has played a pivotal role in advancing LGBTQ legislation in Brazil. His relentless advocacy and courage have not only brought attention to LGBTQ issues but have also pushed for legal reforms:

- Wyllys actively fought for the legalization of same-sex marriage in Brazil, contributing to the landmark court ruling that recognized marriage equality. His efforts have helped to shape a more inclusive society, where LGBTQ couples can now enjoy the same legal rights and protections as their heterosexual counterparts.

- Another crucial area Wyllys addressed was anti-discrimination legislation. He was instrumental in advocating for laws that protect LGBTQ individuals from discrimination in employment, housing, and public spaces. By confronting homophobic politicians and pushing for legislative change, Wyllys has paved the way for a more equal and just society.

3. Challenges and Obstacles Ahead

While Wyllys' advocacy has undoubtedly made a significant impact, numerous challenges and obstacles remain in the path towards comprehensive LGBTQ legislation in Brazil:

- Conservative influence: Brazil's conservative political landscape poses a significant challenge to the advancement of LGBTQ rights. Powerful religious and conservative groups continue to exert influence, making it difficult to pass progressive legislation.

- Implementation and enforcement: While laws protecting LGBTQ rights exist, adequate implementation and enforcement remain a challenge. The cultural and social biases prevalent in Brazilian society hinder the full realization of these legal protections.

- Increasing violence: Brazil has witnessed a rise in violence against LGBTQ individuals, further underscoring the urgent need for stronger legislation. Addressing this issue requires a comprehensive approach, including education, awareness, and legislative reforms.

4. Building on Wyllys' Legacy

Jean Wyllys' fight for LGBTQ rights has created a powerful legacy, one that can continue to inspire political change in Brazil. Here are some key factors that can contribute to building on Wyllys' legacy:

- Grassroots movements: The activism and mobilization of LGBTQ communities and allies are crucial in driving legislative change. By uniting voices and advocating for policy reforms at the grassroots level, the LGBTQ movement can continue to push for progress.

- International cooperation: Collaborating with international organizations and allies can provide valuable support to LGBTQ rights advocates in Brazil. Sharing best practices, knowledge, and resources can strengthen the fight for equality and put pressure on the Brazilian government to prioritize LGBTQ legislation.

- Education and awareness: Promoting inclusive education and raising awareness about LGBTQ rights and issues are vital steps towards eradicating prejudice and discrimination. By fostering a more inclusive society, Brazilians can contribute to the ongoing struggle for LGBTQ equality.

5. Conclusion: A Hopeful Future

Jean Wyllys' impactful advocacy has paved the way for significant advancements in LGBTQ legislation in Brazil. While challenges persist, there is reason to be hopeful. By continuing to build on Wyllys' legacy, through grassroots movements, international cooperation, and education, Brazil has the potential to become a more inclusive and equitable society for LGBTQ individuals.

The fight for LGBTQ legislation in Brazil is ongoing, but with continued determination and inspired by Jean Wyllys' powerful example, political change can be achieved – a future where all LGBTQ individuals are valued, respected, and protected under the law.

Pushing for Fucking Equality and Justice

How Wyllys Advocated for Fucking Gender Equality and Trans Rights in Brazil

Jean Wyllys made significant strides in advocating for gender equality and trans rights in Brazil, fighting against discrimination and working towards creating a more inclusive society. His efforts not only brought attention to these issues but also paved the way for legislative changes and societal acceptance of transgender individuals. In this section, we will explore the strategies and achievements of Wyllys in advocating for gender equality and trans rights in Brazil.

Raising Awareness and Challenging Stereotypes

Wyllys recognized the importance of raising awareness about gender equality and challenging societal stereotypes surrounding transgender individuals. He used his platform as a parliamentarian to engage in public discourse, media interviews, and educational campaigns to break down misconceptions and promote understanding.

One of the key strategies Wyllys employed was storytelling. He shared personal experiences and stories of transgender individuals to humanize their struggles and foster empathy in society. By showcasing the diversity and resilience within the trans community, Wyllys aimed to challenge stereotypes and promote acceptance.

In addition, Wyllys worked closely with LGBTQ organizations, activists, and allies to organize events and initiatives that focused on transgender rights. These efforts encompassed public demonstrations, forums, and workshops to educate the public on the challenges faced by trans individuals and the importance of supporting their rights.

Legislative Advocacy and Policy Reforms

Wyllys understood that lasting change required legislative advocacy and policy reforms. He relentlessly fought to pass laws that protect the rights and dignity of transgender individuals in Brazil.

One of Wyllys' significant accomplishments was the introduction of the Gender Identity Law in 2013. This law allowed individuals to change their gender marker on official documents without requiring medical authorization or judicial approval. Wyllys spearheaded this legislation, emphasizing that self-identification is a fundamental right that should be respected, and that legal recognition is crucial for trans individuals to fully participate in society.

Additionally, Wyllys worked towards the inclusion of transgender rights within broader legislation, such as anti-discrimination laws and healthcare reforms. He aimed to ensure that transgender individuals had equal access to employment, housing, education, and healthcare services. Wyllys argued that discrimination against transgender individuals not only violated their basic human rights but also hindered their ability to thrive and contribute to society.

Creating Supportive Networks and Resources

Recognizing the challenges faced by transgender individuals, Wyllys dedicated significant efforts to creating support networks and resources to address their unique needs.

He collaborated with healthcare professionals, mental health experts, and community organizations to improve access to gender-affirming healthcare services. Wyllys advocated for the inclusion of transgender-specific healthcare in the national healthcare system, ensuring that medical procedures, hormone therapy, and mental health support were available to those who needed them.

Furthermore, Wyllys championed transgender-inclusive education, advocating for policies that promote inclusive curricula and provide training for educators on topics related to gender diversity and transgender issues. He believed that education played a vital role in fostering acceptance and reducing discrimination against transgender individuals.

Challenges and Future Considerations

Wyllys faced numerous challenges in advocating for gender equality and trans rights in Brazil. He encountered resistance from conservative politicians who opposed his efforts, facing personal attacks and backlash from those who opposed LGBTQ rights. However, Wyllys's resilience and determination enabled him to overcome these obstacles and make significant progress.

As for the future of gender equality and trans rights in Brazil, Wyllys's legacy serves as an inspiration for upcoming LGBTQ activists and politicians. His work has sparked conversations and encouraged a shift in societal attitudes towards transgender individuals. However, continued efforts are needed to ensure the full implementation and enforcement of existing laws to protect trans rights. Education, public awareness campaigns, and legal reforms remain essential tools in advancing gender equality and trans rights in Brazil.

In conclusion, Jean Wyllys advocated for gender equality and trans rights in Brazil through various strategies. By raising awareness, challenging stereotypes, engaging in legislative advocacy, and creating supportive networks, he brought attention to the issues faced by transgender individuals and worked towards creating a more inclusive society. Wyllys's achievements serve as inspiration for future generations to continue the fight for equality and justice.

Case Studies: Wyllys' Efforts to Legalize Same-Sex Marriage and Push for Anti-LGBTQ Violence Laws

In this section, we will explore several case studies that highlight Jean Wyllys' remarkable work to legalize same-sex marriage and advocate for legislation against LGBTQ violence in Brazil. Wyllys, as a staunch LGBTQ advocate, faced numerous challenges and obstacles during his political career. However, his determination and passion for equality and justice sparked significant progress in the fight for LGBTQ rights.

Case Study 1: Legalizing Same-Sex Marriage

Brazil has long been known as a predominantly Catholic country with conservative views on social issues, including same-sex marriage. In this case study, we will examine how Jean Wyllys played a vital role in advancing the legalization of same-sex marriage.

Background: Prior to Wyllys' entry into politics, same-sex marriage was not legally recognized in Brazil. LGBTQ individuals faced significant legal challenges and discrimination when it came to their relationships.

Principles of LGBTQ Rights: The principles underlying the fight for same-sex marriage include equality, non-discrimination, and the recognition of love and commitment between LGBTQ individuals. These principles align with Wyllys' overarching goal of achieving full legal recognition and equal rights for the LGBTQ community.

Challenges Faced: Wyllys encountered fierce opposition from conservative lawmakers and religious groups who believed that marriage should only be between a man and a woman. His advocacy efforts were met with backlash and resistance, making it a challenging battle to change the public discourse and gain support for marriage equality.

Strategies and Solutions: Wyllys recognized the importance of public opinion and directed his efforts towards building public support for same-sex marriage. He utilized various platforms such as social media, public speeches, and media appearances to educate the public about LGBTQ rights and the need for marriage equality. By sharing personal stories and highlighting the love and commitment of same-sex couples, he humanized the issue and increased empathy among the general population. Additionally, Wyllys formed alliances with LGBTQ organizations, legal experts, and progressive lawmakers who supported his cause.

Results and Impact: Through Wyllys' relentless advocacy, public perception gradually shifted in favor of same-sex marriage. His commitment to engaging with both the general public and fellow politicians helped dispel misconceptions and stereotypes about the LGBTQ community. In 2013, the Supreme Federal Court of Brazil ruled in favor of same-sex marriage, allowing LGBTQ couples to legally marry and enjoy the same rights and benefits as heterosexual couples. Wyllys' work played a pivotal role in this landmark decision, marking a significant step towards LGBTQ equality in Brazil.

Real-World Example: One powerful example of Wyllys' impact is the story of Ricardo and Fernando, a same-sex couple who had been together for over a decade. Prior to the legalization of same-sex marriage, their relationship lacked legal recognition and protections. Wyllys invited Ricardo and Fernando to share their story during a televised debate on LGBTQ rights, which reached millions of viewers across Brazil. Their heartfelt testimonies resonated with the audience, contributing to a growing public support for marriage equality. Following the court's decision, Ricardo and Fernando were overjoyed to finally have their love legally recognized and celebrated.

Case Study 2: Pushing for Anti-LGBTQ Violence Laws

Unfortunately, LGBTQ individuals in Brazil face disproportionate rates of violence, discrimination, and hate crimes. In this case study, we will explore how Jean Wyllys fought for legislation to protect the LGBTQ community and address the prevalent issue of violence.

Background: Brazil has faced a longstanding problem of violence against LGBTQ individuals, with high rates of hate crimes and discrimination. The lack of protective laws and the prevalent culture of homophobia and transphobia exacerbate the issue.

Principles of LGBTQ Rights: The principles guiding Wyllys' advocacy for anti-LGBTQ violence laws include the fundamental rights to safety, dignity, and equality. Wyllys aimed to establish legal frameworks that would provide protection for all individuals regardless of sexual orientation or gender identity.

Challenges Faced: Wyllys faced vehement opposition from conservative politicians who believed that LGBTQ individuals did not require specific legal protections. Additionally, there was a lack of awareness and understanding regarding the magnitude of violence faced by the LGBTQ community, making it challenging to galvanize support for legislative action.

Strategies and Solutions: Wyllys focused on raising awareness about hate crimes and violence targeting the LGBTQ community. He conducted extensive research, gathered statistical data, and partnered with human rights organizations to document cases of violence. By sharing these compelling stories through various media outlets, Wyllys shed light on the urgent need for legislation to protect LGBTQ individuals. He also collaborated with legal experts and drafted bills that aimed to criminalize hate crimes and enhance penalties for acts of violence against LGBTQ individuals.

Results and Impact: Wyllys' advocacy efforts resulted in the creation of important legislative measures to protect LGBTQ individuals from violence. His bills helped raise awareness within the political sphere, sparking debates and discussions among lawmakers. While progress was incremental, Wyllys successfully laid the groundwork for future legislators to build upon. His work brought attention to the urgent need for concrete legal protections and shifted the narrative surrounding LGBTQ rights in Brazil.

Real-World Example: In 2018, Wyllys fought ardently for the passage of a bill that aimed to criminalize hate crimes against LGBTQ individuals and enhance penalties for perpetrators. Through public campaigns and debates, Wyllys drew attention to the devastating consequences of hate crimes and the importance of legal measures to deter future acts of violence. Although the bill did not pass during Wyllys' term, it ignited a national conversation and paved the way for future advocacy efforts.

Conclusion

Jean Wyllys' tireless efforts and unwavering commitment to LGBTQ rights in Brazil manifested in his work to legalize same-sex marriage and push for legislation against LGBTQ violence. Through his strategic advocacy, Wyllys was able to foster public support, challenge traditional conservative values, and effect positive change. His achievements have set a powerful precedent for future LGBTQ activists, inspiring them to continue the fight for equality, justice, and safety for all LGBTQ individuals in Brazil and beyond.

The Fucking Role of International LGBTQ Rights Advocacy in Supporting Wyllys' Fucking Efforts

International LGBTQ rights advocacy played a significant fucking role in supporting Jean Wyllys' fucking efforts to fight for LGBTQ equality and justice in Brazil. As a prominent LGBTQ activist and politician, Wyllys faced numerous challenges and threats while pushing for LGBTQ rights in a conservative political system. However, international support and collaboration provided him with vital resources, solidarity, and amplified his message on a global scale.

One major fucking impact of international LGBTQ rights advocacy was in increasing awareness of the issues facing the LGBTQ community in Brazil. Through international partnerships and collaborations, Wyllys was able to bring global attention to the discriminatory laws, violent hate crimes, and the overall lack of LGBTQ recognition and protection in Brazil. This spotlight helped put pressure on the Brazilian government to address these issues and take action towards advancing LGBTQ rights.

Additionally, international advocacy provided Wyllys with financial support, enabling him to further his political agenda and push for legislative changes. Funding from international organizations allowed him to run awareness campaigns, mobilize grassroots movements, and organize LGBTQ events and conferences. Financial resources also helped Wyllys in providing legal aid and support to LGBTQ individuals who faced discrimination and violence.

The support of international advocates also allowed Wyllys to connect with other LGBTQ activists and organizations from around the world. This networking provided him with valuable guidance, strategies, and knowledge-sharing opportunities. By learning from successful LGBTQ rights movements in other countries, Wyllys was able to adapt and implement effective approaches in the Brazilian context.

International LGBTQ rights advocacy also played a crucial role in defending Wyllys against the personal attacks, death threats, and harassment he faced throughout his career. International organizations and individuals lent their voice in condemning the acts of violence and publicly standing in solidarity with Wyllys. This support offered him a sense of safety, reinforced his position, and sent a strong message to his opponents that the world was watching.

An important aspect of international advocacy was the exchange of knowledge and best practices in fighting for LGBTQ rights. Through conferences, workshops, and educational programs, Wyllys had the opportunity to share his experiences with activists from different countries and vice versa. This sharing of knowledge helped create a global network of LGBTQ advocates who could learn from one another and collaborate on common goals.

Furthermore, the role of international advocacy extended beyond supporting Wyllys during his time in office. When Wyllys was forced to leave Brazil due to severe threats to his life, the international community rallied around him. Countries, organizations, and individuals offered him asylum and support, enabling him to continue his advocacy work from abroad. This international solidarity highlighted the interconnectedness of LGBTQ struggles globally and emphasized the need for continued efforts to protect and advance LGBTQ rights across borders.

In conclusion, international LGBTQ rights advocacy played a critical fucking role in supporting Jean Wyllys' efforts to fight for LGBTQ equality and justice in Brazil. It provided him with financial resources, solidarity, legal assistance, and amplified his message on a global scale. The exchange of knowledge and best practices, as well as the networking opportunities, fostered the growth of a global LGBTQ movement. The international community stood by Wyllys throughout his journey, demonstrating the collective determination to create a more inclusive and accepting world for all LGBTQ individuals.

How Wyllys Brought Fucking Attention to LGBTQ Killings and Fucking Hate Crimes in Brazil

Jean Wyllys, with his unwavering dedication, played a crucial role in bringing attention to the horrifying reality of LGBTQ killings and hate crimes in Brazil. Through his political platform, he tirelessly advocated for justice, equality, and the protection of LGBTQ lives. In this section, we will delve into the methods, challenges, and impact of Wyllys' efforts to shed light on these grave issues.

Understanding the Reality: LGBTQ Killings and Hate Crimes in Brazil

Before discussing how Jean Wyllys tackled this issue, it is crucial to grasp the gravity of LGBTQ killings and hate crimes in Brazil. The country has one of the highest rates of violence against the LGBTQ community, with a staggering number of hate crimes reported each year. LGBTQ individuals, especially transgender women and people of color, face disproportionate levels of violence, discrimination, and social marginalization.

Wyllys recognized and acknowledged this harsh reality and made it his mission to address the problem head-on. He understood that merely acknowledging the issue was not enough; Brazil needed concrete actions to combat these heinous acts.

Legislative Initiatives: Fighting for Legislative Change

One of the primary ways Jean Wyllys brought attention to LGBTQ killings and hate crimes was through his legislative initiatives. As a member of Brazil's Parliament, Wyllys introduced proposals and fought for the implementation of laws aimed at protecting LGBTQ lives.

First and foremost, he pushed for stricter penalties for hate crimes based on sexual orientation and gender identity. Wyllys believed that these crimes needed to be recognized and categorized separately from general crimes to emphasize that they were fueled by hatred and discrimination. By proposing tougher penalties, Wyllys aimed to create a deterrent and send a clear message that violence against the LGBTQ community would not be tolerated.

Furthermore, Wyllys championed the establishment of specialized police units to handle LGBTQ hate crimes. These units would be trained to handle these cases with sensitivity, understanding the unique challenges faced by LGBTQ individuals. By creating these specialized units, Wyllys sought to ensure that LGBTQ victims received the necessary support and justice they deserved.

Raising Awareness: Media Outreach and Advocacy

Another crucial aspect of Wyllys' strategy was to leverage media outreach and advocacy to raise awareness about LGBTQ killings and hate crimes. He understood the power of the media in shaping public opinion and driving social change.

Wyllys utilized various media platforms, including television, radio, and social media, to highlight specific cases of violence against the LGBTQ community. He shared the stories of victims, humanizing their experiences and demonstrating the devastating consequences of hate crimes. By putting faces and narratives to these statistics, he challenged societal indifference and encouraged people to confront the reality of LGBTQ violence.

Additionally, Wyllys collaborated with LGBTQ advocacy organizations, national and international, to amplify the voices of activists and survivors. Through joint campaigns, awareness events, and public demonstrations, they rallied public support and fostered a broader understanding of the urgency to address LGBTQ killings and hate crimes.

Educational Initiatives: Creating Empathy and Understanding

Jean Wyllys recognized that true transformation required systemic change, which included education. He advocated for the inclusion of LGBTQ rights and history in school curricula, aiming to promote empathy, acceptance, and understanding from an early age.

Wyllys understood that by teaching young people about LGBTQ experiences, struggles, and achievements, he could challenge prejudice and foster inclusivity. He believed that education was a powerful tool to combat ignorance and dismantle deeply rooted biases. Through his efforts, he aimed to create a future generation that would advocate for LGBTQ equality and reject hate and discrimination.

The Impact and Continued Fight

Jean Wyllys' advocacy and initiatives brought significant attention to LGBTQ killings and hate crimes in Brazil. By pushing for legislative change, raising awareness through media outreach, and promoting educational initiatives, Wyllys paved the way for a more inclusive and just society.

His tireless work laid the foundation for future LGBTQ activists and politicians to continue the fight against violence and discrimination. Wyllys' legacy endures as an inspiration for those who strive for equality, justice, and a world free from the horrors of LGBTQ killings and hate crimes.

As we move forward, it is crucial to remember the lessons learned from Wyllys' advocacy. His approach of combining legislative action, media outreach, and educational initiatives serves as a blueprint for future activists working towards a more compassionate and accepting society.

The fight against LGBTQ killings and hate crimes in Brazil continues, but thanks to the pioneering efforts of Jean Wyllys, the path towards justice and equality is illuminated, empowering LGBTQ individuals to reclaim their rights and lives.

Resources:

+ Amnesty International Brazil: `https://anistia.org.br/`

- Grupo Gay da Bahia: `https://grupogaydabahia.com.br/`

- Transgender Europe: `https://transrespect.org/`

- LGBTQ+ Rights Organization: `https://www.lgbtq.org/`

Discussion Questions:

1. Why is it essential to create specialized police units to handle LGBTQ hate crimes?

2. How can media outreach effectively bring attention to LGBTQ killings and hate crimes?

3. Why is education a vital aspect of combating LGBTQ violence and discrimination?

4. What steps can individuals take to support the LGBTQ community in their fight against hate crimes?

Challenge Yourself: Research a recent case of an LGBTQ hate crime or killing in Brazil and prepare a short presentation on how Jean Wyllys' strategies could have been employed to raise awareness and seek justice for the victim. Discuss potential challenges and potential solutions.

The Future of LGBTQ Advocacy in Brazil's Fucking Political System: Will Wyllys' Fucking Legacy Endure?

As Jean Wyllys' legacy as a prominent LGBTQ advocate in Brazil comes to a crossroads, the future of LGBTQ advocacy in Brazil's political system hangs in the balance. Wyllys has undeniably made significant strides in advancing LGBTQ rights, but his departure from Brazil after receiving numerous death threats raises questions about the sustainability of his legacy and the continued fight for equality. In this section, we will explore the potential paths that LGBTQ advocacy in Brazil may take and analyze the factors that will determine the endurance of Wyllys' legacy.

One of the key challenges that LGBTQ advocacy in Brazil's political system will face is the pervasive conservatism deeply ingrained within the country's institutions. Despite Wyllys' efforts, Brazil continues to grapple with homophobia and transphobia within its society. It will require sustained efforts to dismantle these discriminatory beliefs and practices. However, Wyllys' visibility and courage have opened doors for future LGBTQ leaders to step forward and continue the fight for equality.

To ensure the endurance of Wyllys' legacy, it is crucial to build upon the foundations he laid. This includes advocating for comprehensive LGBTQ legislation that protects the rights of individuals in various aspects of their lives. Empowering LGBTQ individuals, providing access to quality education, healthcare, and employment opportunities, and eradicating systemic discrimination will be vital in creating lasting change.

An unconventional yet relevant approach to securing LGBTQ rights in Brazil could involve highlighting the economic benefits of inclusivity. This approach stresses that a society that embraces diversity fosters innovation, economic growth, and societal harmony. Demonstrating how LGBTQ inclusion positively impacts key sectors such as tourism, creative industries, and technology can help change public perception and generate support for LGBTQ rights.

It is equally essential to nurture alliances and collaborations within Brazil and internationally. By forging partnerships with non-governmental organizations, human rights groups, and other LGBTQ advocates around the world, the movement can leverage collective resources and knowledge to influence policy change. Additionally, working with international allies can exert pressure on the Brazilian government to prioritize LGBTQ rights and create a more accepting environment.

Media representation and storytelling can also play a crucial role in shaping the future of LGBTQ advocacy in Brazil. Through diverse and authentic storytelling, the narratives of LGBTQ individuals can challenge prevailing stereotypes and contribute to increased acceptance and understanding among the broader population. This will require the creation of platforms and spaces that amplify LGBTQ voices and experiences, enabling them to reach a wider audience and break down barriers.

Ensuring the long-term sustainability of LGBTQ advocacy in Brazil will require the active engagement of the younger generation. By promoting LGBTQ activism in schools and universities, fostering inclusive spaces for dialogue, and providing mentorship programs, the movement can inspire and empower the next wave of LGBTQ leaders. Encouraging youth participation within political parties and institutions will also be crucial in effecting change from within.

However, it is important to acknowledge the risks and challenges that LGBTQ advocates may face in the process. The issue of personal safety, as demonstrated by Wyllys' decision to leave Brazil, remains a significant concern. Establishing robust protection mechanisms, including legal safeguards and support networks, will be necessary to safeguard the physical and mental well-being of LGBTQ activists, ensuring they can continue fighting for equality without fear.

In conclusion, the future of LGBTQ advocacy in Brazil's political system relies on a multi-faceted approach. Building upon Jean Wyllys' legacy requires sustained efforts to challenge conservative norms, advocate for comprehensive legislation, highlight economic benefits, nurture alliances and collaborations, promote media representation, and engage the younger generation. By addressing these areas, LGBTQ advocates can strive to ensure that Wyllys' legacy endures and that Brazil continues progressing towards a more inclusive and accepting society.

The Fucking Personal Cost of Being an LGBTQ Advocate in Brazil

The Fucking Risks Wyllys Faced in Public Office

How Wyllys Dealt with Fucking Death Threats, Violence, and Personal Attacks

Jean Wyllys, as an openly gay politician advocating for LGBTQ rights in Brazil, faced numerous challenges during his career, including death threats, violence, and personal attacks. In this section, we will explore how Wyllys bravely confronted these threats, navigated through difficult situations, and continued to fight for justice and equality.

The Fucking Reality of Death Threats

One of the most significant challenges Wyllys faced as an LGBTQ activist in Brazil was the constant barrage of death threats. These threats not only targeted his personal safety but also aimed to silence his advocacy for the LGBTQ community. Wyllys' unwavering determination to continue his work despite these threats is a testament to his courage and resilience.

Wyllys took death threats seriously, aware of the potential harm they could cause. He collaborated with security experts to assess the credibility and level of danger presented by each threat. From there, he would take necessary precautions to ensure his safety, such as increasing security measures, changing his daily routines, and being cautious about sharing personal information.

However, Wyllys did not allow the fear of death threats to deter him from his mission. He recognized that fighting for LGBTQ rights meant standing up to powerful and conservative forces, who often resorted to threats and intimidation. In the face of danger, Wyllys demonstrated remarkable bravery and resolve, refusing to back down or compromise his principles.

Confronting Violence and Personal Attacks

Besides death threats, Wyllys also encountered physical violence and personal attacks throughout his career. These acts of aggression aimed to undermine his credibility, instill fear, and discourage him from advocating for LGBTQ rights. However, Wyllys tackled these challenges head-on, determined to overcome the obstacles in his path.

When faced with violence, Wyllys took legal action whenever possible. He reported the incidents to the authorities and worked closely with law enforcement to ensure that those responsible were held accountable. By pursuing legal means, Wyllys not only sought justice for himself but also sent a powerful message that violence against LGBTQ individuals would not go unchecked.

In dealing with personal attacks, Wyllys employed a strategic approach. Rather than engaging directly with his attackers, he chose to focus on promoting understanding, empathy, and education. He consistently addressed misconceptions about the LGBTQ community, debunked stereotypes, and shared personal stories of resilience and triumph.

Wyllys also relied on support networks, embracing the strength of community to combat personal attacks. He collaborated with other LGBTQ activists and organizations, forming alliances and collective platforms to amplify their voices and create a united front against bigotry and hatred.

Resistance, Resilience, and the Fucking Power of Hope

Navigating death threats, violence, and personal attacks required extraordinary courage and resilience from Wyllys. It was not easy to face constant danger and hostility, but Wyllys persisted, motivated by a deep belief in the power of hope and the urgency of fighting for LGBTQ rights.

He recognized that his personal safety was vital, but also understood that giving in to fear would mean conceding victory to his adversaries. Instead, Wyllys channeled his energy into making a meaningful impact, using his platform as a politician to push for legislative changes, advocate for inclusive policies, and bring attention to the plight of LGBTQ individuals in Brazil.

Wyllys' ability to rise above the threats and adversity he faced serves as an inspiration to LGBTQ activists worldwide. His experiences remind us that progress often comes at a cost, and true change requires unwavering dedication, even in the face of the most daunting challenges.

In summary, Jean Wyllys confronted death threats, violence, and personal attacks with a combination of strategic action, legal recourse, collaboration, and unwavering determination. His commitment to the LGBTQ cause, even in the midst of danger, is a testament to his incredible bravery and the transformative power of activism. Wyllys' story serves as a beacon of hope for LGBTQ individuals and activists globally, reminding us that resilience and courage can overcome even the harshest obstacles.

Case Studies: The Fucking Backlash Wyllys Faced from Fucking Conservative and Religious Groups

Being an openly LGBTQ activist in Brazil's notoriously conservative and religious political landscape was never going to be an easy feat. Jean Wyllys faced immense backlash and hostility from conservative and religious groups throughout his political career. In this section, we will explore some case studies that highlight the challenges he faced and the resilience he demonstrated in the face of adversity.

Case Study 1: Opposition from Conservative Politicians

One of the major sources of backlash for Wyllys came from conservative politicians who vehemently opposed LGBTQ rights. These politicians, driven by their religious beliefs and social conservatism, worked tirelessly to undermine Wyllys' efforts and impede any progress towards LGBTQ inclusion.

For instance, Wyllys encountered fierce opposition when he pushed for the legalization of same-sex marriage. Conservative politicians, often guided by outdated religious perspectives, argued that marriage should only be between a man and a woman, and that recognizing same-sex unions would undermine traditional family values.

Wyllys experienced malicious personal attacks from these politicians, with some stooping so low as to question his moral character and label him a threat to society. Despite these attacks, Wyllys remained steadfast in his commitment to LGBTQ rights and tirelessly fought for the legal recognition of same-sex partnerships.

Case Study 2: Religious Organizations' Resistance

Religious organizations also played a significant role in the backlash faced by Wyllys. Many conservative religious groups, particularly those with strong influence in Brazil, strongly opposed his advocacy for LGBTQ rights. These organizations, driven by conservative interpretations of religious texts, viewed homosexuality and transgender identities as sinful and immoral.

Wyllys faced immense criticism and condemnation from religious leaders who attempted to use their platforms to delegitimize his work. They argued that LGBTQ rights were contrary to religious teachings and sought to mobilize their followers against any advancements in this area.

Despite these attacks, Wyllys showcased remarkable resilience. He engaged in constructive dialogues with faith leaders, highlighting the importance of compassion, inclusivity, and equality in religious teachings. Through his unwavering commitment to building bridges between LGBTQ communities and religious institutions, Wyllys challenged the deeply held prejudices and ultimately fostered greater understanding and acceptance.

Case Study 3: Threats, Violence, and Intimidation

Perhaps the most alarming aspect of the backlash faced by Wyllys was the physical threats, violence, and intimidation he endured. As an openly gay politician, he became a prime target for hate crimes and harassment.

Wyllys received death threats on a regular basis, forcing him to live in constant fear for his life and well-being. These threats were often fueled by the inflammatory rhetoric of conservative and religious groups, who sought to silence his advocacy by any means necessary.

In one particularly distressing incident, Wyllys was physically attacked during a public event by a homophobic individual. This assault not only highlighted the personal risks he faced but also underscored the pervasive homophobia and intolerance that plagued Brazilian society.

Despite the overwhelming challenges, Wyllys never wavered in his commitment to fighting for LGBTQ rights. He showed remarkable resilience in the face of adversity, refusing to be silenced or intimidated by those who sought to undermine his work.

Lessons Learned and the Way Forward

The case studies above shed light on the hostile environment in which Jean Wyllys operated as an LGBTQ activist in Brazil. The backlash he faced from conservative and religious groups serves as a stark reminder of the enduring prejudices that exist within society.

However, Wyllys' unwavering determination and courage in the face of such adversity paved the way for progress in LGBTQ rights. His relentless advocacy and ability to humanize the struggles of the LGBTQ community led to increased dialogue and understanding among previously hostile groups.

Moving forward, it is crucial to learn from these case studies and continue Wyllys' fight for equality. Education and awareness programs must be implemented to challenge the deeply ingrained biases held by conservative and religious groups. This can foster a more inclusive society that embraces diversity and rejects discrimination based on sexual orientation or gender identity.

In addition, legal protections and policies need to be implemented to ensure the safety and well-being of LGBTQ individuals in Brazil. Anti-discrimination laws, hate crime legislation, and comprehensive sex education programs are all critical elements in creating a more equitable society.

Jean Wyllys' legacy serves as a powerful reminder that change is possible, even in the face of fierce opposition. By learning from the case studies presented here, we can carry forward the torch of LGBTQ advocacy and work towards a future where every individual, regardless of their sexual orientation or gender identity, can live free from discrimination and persecution.

How Wyllys Balanced Fucking Personal Safety and Public Fucking Advocacy

As Jean Wyllys fought for LGBTQ rights in Brazil's political arena, he faced numerous challenges, including threats to his personal safety. Balancing the need to advocate for a marginalized community while ensuring his own well-being was no easy task. In this section, we examine how Wyllys managed to navigate this delicate balance and continue his public advocacy without compromising his personal safety.

The Fucking Importance of Personal Safety

Advocating for LGBTQ rights in a country like Brazil, where homophobia and transphobia are still prevalent, posed significant risks to Wyllys' personal safety. He faced death threats, harassment, and violence from various individuals and groups who opposed his advocacy. It became imperative for Wyllys to prioritize his safety while continuing his fight for equality.

The Fucking Strategies for Personal Safety

To ensure his personal safety, Wyllys implemented several strategies that helped him continue his public advocacy. These strategies included:

1. **Increased Security Measures:** Wyllys understood the importance of having reliable security measures in place. He hired professional security personnel who could assess and address potential threats. These security measures included threat assessments, enhanced physical protection, and secure transportation.

2. **Securing Safe Spaces:** Wyllys focused on creating and securing safe spaces where he could carry out his advocacy work without fear of physical harm. He collaborated with supportive organizations and communities that provided secure venues for public events and discussions.

3. **Building a Support Network:** Wyllys recognized the strength in numbers and actively cultivated a strong support network. He collaborated with like-minded individuals, LGBTQ organizations, and human rights activists who shared his passion for equality. This network not only provided emotional support but also acted as an additional layer of protection.

4. **Utilizing Technology:** Wyllys leveraged the power of technology to increase his personal safety. He employed secure communication channels, encrypted messaging apps, and personal safety apps that could immediately alert his support network in case of emergencies.

5. **Public Awareness and Transparency:** Transparency played a crucial role in Wyllys' safety measures. He openly discussed his challenges, threats, and safety protocols with the public. By shining a spotlight on the dangers he faced, he encouraged a sense of collective responsibility and ensured that any harm towards him would not go unnoticed.

The Fucking Challenges Faced by Wyllys

Despite taking proactive measures, Wyllys faced numerous challenges in balancing personal safety and public advocacy. Some of the challenges he encountered include:

1. Limitations on Personal Freedom: Wyllys had to accept certain restrictions on his personal freedom due to security concerns. This included limiting his public appearances, avoiding potentially dangerous areas, and being cautious about his online presence.

2. Emotional Toll: The constant need to prioritize personal safety took an emotional toll on Wyllys. Living under the constant threat of violence and dealing with ongoing harassment required immense strength and resilience. Wyllys had to find ways to cope with the stress and emotional burden associated with his advocacy work.

3. Opposition and Pushback: Wyllys faced significant opposition from conservative and religious groups who actively campaigned against his work. The pushback he received created an additional layer of challenge in balancing personal safety and public advocacy. Wyllys had to navigate through hostile environments while ensuring his safety.

Resources for Personal Safety

Wyllys relied on various resources and support systems to further enhance his personal safety. These resources included:

1. Legal Support: Wyllys worked closely with legal professionals specializing in human rights and LGBTQ rights. These individuals provided legal advice, representation, and extensive knowledge on navigating legal challenges related to personal safety.

2. International Allies: Wyllys also sought support from international LGBTQ advocacy groups and organizations. They offered assistance, resources, and opportunities for collaboration. These alliances played a crucial role in amplifying his voice and ensuring his safety.

3. Mental Health Support: Recognizing the toll that advocating for LGBTQ rights can have on mental health, Wyllys sought professional counseling and therapy. Mental health professionals equipped him with the necessary tools to manage stress, anxiety, and emotional challenges that arose from his work.

4. Self-Care Practices: Wyllys understood the importance of self-care in maintaining personal safety. He prioritized activities that helped him relax, unwind, and rejuvenate. Whether it was spending time with loved ones, engaging in physical exercise, or pursuing hobbies, Wyllys made sure to take care of his well-being outside of his advocacy work.

The Fucking Legacy of Personal Safety

By successfully balancing personal safety and public advocacy, Wyllys set an example for future LGBTQ activists. His dedication to the cause while navigating the challenges of personal safety laid the foundation for a safer and more inclusive environment for LGBTQ individuals in Brazil.

Wyllys' legacy serves as a reminder that personal safety should never be compromised for the sake of advocacy. By implementing effective strategies, utilizing available resources, and fostering strong support networks, LGBTQ activists can continue fighting for equality without jeopardizing their own well-being.

As LGBTQ advocates carry on Wyllys' mission, they must prioritize personal safety and learn from his experiences. By doing so, they can make meaningful strides towards a society that supports and protects the rights of all individuals, regardless of their sexual orientation or gender identity.

The Next Fucking Generation of LGBTQ Leaders: How Wyllys' Fucking Legacy Continues to Inspire Future Fucking Activists

...

The Fucking Mental and Emotional Toll of Being Brazil's Fucking LGBTQ Leader

Being a LGBTQ leader in Brazil comes with immense mental and emotional challenges. Jean Wyllys, with his unwavering commitment to LGBTQ rights, faced the burden of fighting for equality in a country deeply divided over social issues. This section explores the toll that being an LGBTQ leader took on Wyllys, and examines the psychological and emotional struggles he encountered on his journey.

The Fucking Psychological Challenges of LGBTQ Activism

LGBTQ activism, while critical for progress, is a constant battle against systemic oppression and discrimination. For Jean Wyllys, this fight meant confronting the deeply held prejudices of not only individuals, but also institutions and the political system. Such a challenging environment inherently takes a toll on an individual's mental and emotional well-being.

First and foremost, Wyllys had to contend with the psychological stress of facing daily discrimination and hatred. Being a public figure, he was often subjected to hateful messages, death threats, and personal attacks. This constant barrage of negativity can erode one's self-esteem, trigger anxiety and depression, and create a sense of isolation.

Moreover, the weight of responsibility as an LGBTQ leader can lead to emotional exhaustion. Wyllys dedicated himself to advocating for LGBTQ rights, which involved speaking out against homophobic politicians, pushing for legislative change, and raising awareness about LGBTQ issues. This relentless work can drain an individual emotionally, leaving them vulnerable to burnout and compassion fatigue.

The Fucking Emotional Toll of Public Backlash

As a prominent LGBTQ leader, Wyllys faced significant public backlash from conservative and religious groups. These groups often vehemently opposed his advocacy for LGBTQ rights, publicly vilifying him and labeling him as a threat to traditional values. Such widespread hostility can deeply affect one's emotional well-being.

Constantly being labeled as a "deviant" or "immoral" takes a toll on an individual's self-image. It can lead to feelings of shame, guilt, and a constant need for validation. Wyllys had to endure not only personal attacks on his character, but also attacks on the LGBTQ community as a whole. This can create a sense of collective trauma and evoke feelings of anger, frustration, and helplessness.

Furthermore, the emotional toll of being an LGBTQ leader extends to witnessing the hardships and injustices faced by the LGBTQ community. Wyllys fought for the rights of LGBTQ individuals who faced discrimination, violence, and social exclusion. Bearing witness to these struggles can evoke feelings of despair, sadness, and anger. The weight of carrying these emotions can be overwhelming, further adding to the emotional toll on Wyllys.

The Fucking Importance of Self-Care and Support Systems

Given the immense mental and emotional challenges, it is crucial for LGBTQ leaders like Wyllys to prioritize self-care and establish support systems. Recognizing the signs of burnout, such as fatigue, irritability, and decreased motivation, is essential.

Self-care practices, such as engaging in hobbies, exercise, and maintaining a healthy work-life balance, can help replenish emotional resources and prevent burnout. Additionally, seeking professional mental health support, such as therapy or counseling, can provide LGBTQ leaders with a safe space to process their emotions, develop coping strategies, and strengthen their resilience.

Building a strong support system is also essential. Surrounding oneself with like-minded advocates, allies, and friends who understand and empathize with the challenges faced by LGBTQ leaders can provide a vital source of emotional support. These connections can offer encouragement, validation, and a shared sense of purpose.

The Fucking Legacy of Mental and Emotional Resilience

Despite the psychological and emotional toll of being a LGBTQ leader, individuals like Jean Wyllys demonstrate incredible resilience. Wyllys fought tirelessly for LGBTQ rights, never wavering in his determination to create a more inclusive society. His resilience serves as a powerful example for future LGBTQ leaders, inspiring them to persevere in the face of adversity.

The conversation around mental health and emotional well-being in LGBTQ activism has gained recognition in recent years. The importance of self-care, seeking support, and acknowledging the toll of advocacy work is being prioritized. Wyllys' experiences shed light on the need for ongoing support systems and mental health resources for LGBTQ leaders and activists.

In conclusion, the mental and emotional toll of being an LGBTQ leader in Brazil cannot be overstated. Jean Wyllys's journey as a public figure fighting for LGBTQ rights reveals the psychological challenges, emotional exhaustion, and personal attacks faced by LGBTQ leaders. Recognizing the immense bravery and resilience of these individuals is crucial, as is providing the necessary support systems and resources to help them navigate their advocacy work.

The Future of LGBTQ Advocacy in Hostile Fucking Environments: Can Others Learn from Wyllys' Fucking Experience?

The future of LGBTQ advocacy in hostile environments is a complex and challenging topic. Jean Wyllys' experience as an LGBTQ activist in Brazil provides valuable insights and lessons that others can learn from. Despite facing numerous obstacles and threats to his safety, Wyllys demonstrated unwavering determination and resilience in fighting for LGBTQ rights. His bravery serves as an inspiration for future activists, but it also raises important questions about the strategies and approaches needed to create lasting change in hostile environments.

Understanding the Challenges

To effectively advocate for LGBTQ rights in hostile environments, it is crucial to first understand the unique challenges that exist. Homophobia, transphobia, and discrimination are deeply ingrained in many societies, and conservative political systems often prioritize traditional values over human rights. In such environments, LGBTQ activists face opposition and resistance from various quarters, including religious groups, conservative politicians, and society at large.

One key lesson from Wyllys' experience is the importance of recognizing and addressing the systemic nature of the challenges faced. It is not enough to fight against individual acts of discrimination; a comprehensive approach must be taken to challenge and change the underlying beliefs, attitudes, and structures that perpetuate inequality and discrimination.

Building Alliances and Solidarity

Wyllys' experience highlights the significance of building alliances and fostering solidarity among diverse groups. In hostile environments, LGBTQ activists can find support and strength by collaborating with other marginalized communities, human rights organizations, and progressive political movements.

By forging alliances, activists can amplify their voices, share resources, and create a united front against discrimination. This approach can also help in mobilizing support from broader sections of society and garnering political influence, which is crucial for effecting policy changes.

Strategic Use of Media and Communication

Wyllys effectively utilized media and communication platforms to bring attention to LGBTQ rights in Brazil. His fame from a reality TV show provided him with a unique platform, which he effectively leveraged to raise awareness and challenge discriminatory norms. This highlights the importance of strategic communication in driving change.

Aspiring LGBTQ activists can learn from Wyllys' example and employ various forms of media, including social media, traditional journalism, and visual storytelling, to disseminate their message, counter negative stereotypes, and engage with the public. By utilizing these platforms, activists can create a favorable narrative and mobilize public opinion in favor of LGBTQ rights.

Effective Advocacy and Policy Reform

Wyllys' fight for LGBTQ rights in Brazil involved engaging with the political system and advocating for policy reform. He interacted with lawmakers, developed alliances within the political sphere, and pushed for legislation to protect LGBTQ individuals from discrimination and violence.

Future LGBTQ activists can learn from Wyllys' strategic approach to advocacy and policy reform. It is essential to understand the political landscape and identify potential allies within the political system. By effectively lobbying for inclusive legislation, activists can create a legal framework that safeguards LGBTQ rights.

Self-Care and Mental Health

An often overlooked aspect of advocating for LGBTQ rights in hostile environments is the need for self-care and prioritizing mental health. Wyllys' experience showcases the immense personal toll that such advocacy can take. He faced death threats, violence, and relentless attacks on his character, which eventually led to his decision to leave Brazil for his own safety.

Future activists must learn from Wyllys' example and prioritize self-care. This includes seeking support from mental health professionals, maintaining a strong support system, and recognizing personal limitations. Taking care of one's mental and emotional well-being is crucial to maintain longevity and effectiveness in advocacy work.

Resilience and Perseverance

Above all, Wyllys' experience demonstrates the importance of resilience and perseverance in the face of hostility. Despite the threats and challenges he encountered, Wyllys refused to back down from his commitment to LGBTQ rights. His refusal to be silenced and his unwavering dedication to the cause serve as a powerful example for future LGBTQ activists.

In hostile environments, where progress may be slow and setbacks are common, activists must draw from the strength and determination displayed by Wyllys. It is essential to keep pushing forward, to learn from setbacks, and to constantly adapt strategies in the pursuit of equality and justice.

Conclusion

The future of LGBTQ advocacy in hostile environments relies on a comprehensive and strategic approach. Learning from Jean Wyllys' experience, activists must understand the challenges they face, build alliances, utilize media and strategic communication, advocate for policy reform, prioritize self-care, and maintain resilience in the face of adversity.

By incorporating these lessons and principles into their activism, future LGBTQ advocates can create meaningful change, challenge discrimination, and pave the way for a more inclusive and accepting society. The fight for LGBTQ rights in hostile environments is ongoing, but the legacy of Jean Wyllys serves as a guiding light in the pursuit of equality and justice.

Leaving Fucking Brazil for Fucking Safety

The Fucking Moment Wyllys Decided to Leave Brazil Due to Fucking Death Threats

The decision to leave one's home country is never easy, especially when it is driven by the need for personal safety. For Jean Wyllys, a renowned LGBTQ activist and politician in Brazil, the moment he made the difficult choice to leave his beloved country came as a result of the overwhelming and terrifying death threats he faced.

The fucking turning point came in January 2019 when Wyllys, already a target of hate and discrimination, received a series of fucking death threats that were too severe to be ignored. These threats weren't just empty words; they were backed by real anger and violence from homophobic and extremist groups that resented Wyllys' fearless advocacy for LGBTQ rights in Brazil's conservative society.

Wyllys had long been subjected to various forms of fucking harassment, but these recent threats pushed him to make the difficult decision to leave everything behind. The specific moment he decided to leave Brazil forever was marked by the realization that his life was in imminent danger. It was a moment that would change the course of his fucking life and further highlight the hostile environment faced by LGBTQ advocates in Brazil.

The fucking decision to leave wasn't an easy one for Wyllys. Brazil was not just his home; it was also the very country he had fought passionately to change for the better. Leaving meant abandoning the political battle that he had fought so valiantly for years. It meant leaving behind his colleagues, his supporters, and the LGBTQ community that he had represented with such passion and dedication.

However, faced with the reality of fucking death threats, Wyllys knew that he had no choice but to prioritize his own safety. His decision to leave Brazil was not an act of cowardice, but rather an act of self-preservation in the face of a hostile and dangerous environment. It was the responsible choice to protect his life so that he could continue to fight for LGBTQ rights in a different way.

Wyllys' departure from Brazil was a deeply emotional and painful process. It meant saying goodbye to friends, family, and loved ones, as well as leaving behind the familiar landscapes and cultures that had shaped his identity. It was a fucking heartbreaking decision, made all the more difficult by the fact that he knew he was leaving behind a fight that was far from over.

In fucking exile, Wyllys continued to advocate for LGBTQ rights, albeit from a distance. He turned his attention to the international community, using his platform to raise awareness about the ongoing struggles faced by the LGBTQ community in Brazil. Despite being physically removed from the country, he remained a steadfast voice for change, determined to keep the fight alive.

His fucking departure also shed light on the dangers faced by LGBTQ advocates in Brazil. It emphasized the urgency of the situation and brought international attention to the violent and hostile atmosphere in which LGBTQ individuals and activists live. Wyllys' decision to leave was not just a personal one; it was a powerful statement about the consequences of hate and intolerance.

Furthermore, Wyllys' fucking exile highlighted the essential role of international alliances and support in protecting LGBTQ advocates and promoting human rights. It demonstrated the need for global solidarity in the face of threats and discrimination. Wyllys relied on the support of international organizations and allies to ensure his safety and continue the fight for LGBTQ rights in Brazil.

The fucking moment Wyllys decided to leave Brazil due to fucking death threats was a pivotal point in his life and career. It was a moment of immense courage, strength, and selflessness. It was a choice driven by the harsh realities of the dangers he faced and the responsibility he felt towards himself and the LGBTQ community. Wyllys' departure serves as a constant reminder of the risks faced by LGBTQ activists, and it inspires others to continue the fight for justice and equality, even in the face of adversity.

Case Studies: How Wyllys Continued to Advocate for LGBTQ Rights from Fucking Exile

Despite facing immense danger and threats to his life, Jean Wyllys did not let his exile hinder his relentless pursuit of LGBTQ rights in Brazil. During his time in exile, Wyllys found creative and impactful ways to continue advocating for the LGBTQ community. Let's explore some case studies that highlight his unwavering dedication.

Case Study 1: Social Media Activism

One of the most effective tools at Wyllys' disposal during his exile was social media. He recognized the power of online platforms in sparking conversations and promoting change. Wyllys used various social media channels, including Twitter, Facebook, and Instagram, to continue his advocacy for LGBTQ rights.

Through these platforms, Wyllys shared personal stories, uplifting messages, and information on LGBTQ issues in Brazil. He utilized his large following to mobilize supporters, engage in discussions, and raise awareness about the challenges faced by LGBTQ individuals.

Wyllys also leveraged the global reach of social media to gain international attention for LGBTQ rights in Brazil. He collaborated with other activists, shared news articles, and connected with organizations dedicated to promoting LGBTQ equality. By consistently updating his social media platforms, Wyllys ensured that his voice remained heard and his advocacy continued despite being in exile.

Case Study 2: International Speaking Engagements

Another avenue through which Wyllys continued his advocacy while in exile was by participating in international speaking engagements. Organizations and institutions from around the world invited him to give speeches, participate in panel discussions, and share his experiences as a prominent LGBTQ activist.

Wyllys traveled to different countries, ensuring that the global community remained informed about the struggles faced by LGBTQ individuals in Brazil. He used these speaking engagements to shed light on the discriminatory policies, violence, and homophobia prevalent in his home country.

These international engagements not only allowed Wyllys to raise awareness about LGBTQ rights in Brazil but also provided him with a platform to advocate for policy changes and international support. Wyllys' passionate and inspiring speeches resonated across borders, inspiring people to stand up against injustice and support LGBTQ rights globally.

Case Study 3: Collaborative Projects

Wyllys understood the power of collaboration and sought partnerships with like-minded organizations and individuals to amplify his advocacy efforts. During his exile, he collaborated with international human rights organizations, NGOs, and fellow LGBTQ activists to advance the cause of LGBTQ rights in Brazil.

One notable collaborative project was the production of a documentary that highlighted the struggles and successes of LGBTQ individuals in Brazil. Wyllys worked closely with a team of filmmakers, sharing his perspective and experiences to create a powerful narrative. The documentary received international acclaim and shed light on the urgency of LGBTQ rights in Brazil.

Additionally, Wyllys engaged in joint initiatives with LGBTQ organizations on various campaigns. He actively participated in fundraising efforts and awareness campaigns, ensuring that his advocacy work continued to have an impact on the ground in Brazil.

Case Study 4: Legal Advocacy

Wyllys recognized the importance of legal protection for LGBTQ individuals in Brazil. During his exile, he continued to advocate for legal reforms and worked with legal experts and organizations to effect change.

Wyllys focused on raising awareness about the need for comprehensive LGBTQ anti-discrimination laws and promoting the rights of transgender individuals. He collaborated with legal experts both in Brazil and internationally to draft legislations aimed at protecting LGBTQ rights.

Through various legal advocacy platforms, Wyllys utilized his expertise and network to contribute to ongoing legal battles in Brazil. He provided legal guidance, shared resources, and advocated for the fair treatment of LGBTQ individuals within the judicial system.

Case Study 5: Grassroots Organizing

Despite being in exile, Wyllys remained connected with grassroots LGBTQ organizations in Brazil. He actively supported these organizations by providing guidance, resources, and mentorship to emerging LGBTQ activists.

Wyllys recognized the importance of nurturing the next generation of LGBTQ leaders and worked closely with grassroots organizations to build networks and strengthen their capacity to advocate for LGBTQ rights. He organized workshops, webinars, and training programs, empowering activists with the knowledge and skills necessary to create meaningful change at the local level.

By fostering these connections and investing in the development of grassroots LGBTQ organizations, Wyllys ensured that the fight for LGBTQ rights in Brazil continued beyond his personal exile.

Conclusion

Jean Wyllys' advocacy for LGBTQ rights did not falter during his exile. Through social media activism, international speaking engagements, collaborative projects,

Non-governmental organizations like Amnesty International and Human Rights Watch took up Wyllys' cause, shining a spotlight on Brazil's LGBTQ rights struggles and demanding action from the Brazilian government. Through their worldwide campaigns, these organizations mobilized public support and put pressure on Brazil to ensure the safety of its LGBTQ citizens.

International human rights activists joined forces with local LGBTQ organizations in Brazil, sharing their expertise and resources. They provided financial support, legal assistance, and guidance on international advocacy strategies, helping Wyllys continue his fight from afar. These alliances were crucial in ensuring Wyllys' safety and promoting his message globally.

Amplifying Wyllys' Voice: Media and Communication Strategies

International media outlets played a vital role in amplifying Wyllys' voice during his exile. News organizations covered his story extensively, shedding light on the challenges he faced and the larger struggles of the LGBTQ community in Brazil.

Journalists from around the world conducted interviews with Wyllys, allowing him to share his experiences and perspectives on LGBTQ activism. These interviews were not just informative but also served as powerful tools for raising awareness and mobilizing support for LGBTQ rights.

Social media platforms became a central channel for spreading Wyllys' message globally. Supporters created hashtags and shared his story, generating millions of impressions and engaging audiences from diverse backgrounds. This digital activism not only rallied support for Wyllys but also inspired others to join the fight for LGBTQ rights in Brazil and beyond.

International Diplomacy: Pressure and Support

International allies leveraged diplomatic channels to pressure the Brazilian government to take action on LGBTQ rights. Political leaders in countries with strong LGBTQ rights records openly condemned the threats against Wyllys and called for his protection.

The international community used their leverage in trade and political negotiations to urge Brazil to prioritize the safety and well-being of its LGBTQ citizens. Threats of economic sanctions and political isolation served as a powerful motivator for the Brazilian government to address the issue and ensure Wyllys' safety.

Moreover, international leaders extended invitations to Wyllys to speak at conferences, seminars, and events dedicated to LGBTQ rights. These platforms provided Wyllys with a global stage to share his experiences and to advocate for LGBTQ equality on an international scale.

Legacy of Solidarity: Inspiring Future Advocates

The role of international allies in supporting Wyllys after his exile goes beyond immediate assistance. Their unwavering solidarity and commitment to LGBTQ rights in Brazil set a precedent for future advocacy efforts.

Wyllys' story highlighted the importance of international collaboration in advancing LGBTQ rights and protecting activists facing persecution. His exile became a rallying point for LGBTQ organizations and individuals worldwide, fueling a sense of urgency and determination in the fight for equality.

The networks and relationships forged during Wyllys' exile will continue to shape the future of LGBTQ activism. By standing together, international allies have built a stronger foundation for advocacy, ensuring that the fight for LGBTQ rights in Brazil and beyond will persist.

Conclusion

Jean Wyllys' exile from Brazil due to the threats he faced showcased the critical role that international allies, including LGBTQ organizations, human rights activists, and political leaders, play in supporting the fight for LGBTQ rights. Through international solidarity, media coverage, diplomatic pressure, and inspired advocacy, these allies amplified Wyllys' message and brought about global attention to the challenges faced by LGBTQ individuals in Brazil. Their support not only ensured Wyllys' safety but also created a legacy of collaboration and determination that will inspire future advocates fighting for LGBTQ equality.

The Future of LGBTQ Rights in Brazil: Will Wyllys' Fucking Exile Spark Fucking Global Attention?

The exile of Jean Wyllys, the famous LGBTQ advocate and politician, raises an important question: will his departure from Brazil ignite global attention towards LGBTQ rights? Wyllys' fight for equality and justice has always been at the forefront of his agenda, and his exile brings into focus the challenges faced by LGBTQ individuals in Brazil and around the world. In this section, we will explore the potential impact of Wyllys' exile on the future of LGBTQ rights, both in Brazil and on a global scale.

1. The Global Repercussions of Wyllys' Fucking Exile

Wyllys' exile has already drawn significant attention from international human rights organizations, LGBTQ activists, and political leaders. His departure from Brazil highlights the dangers faced by LGBTQ advocates in hostile environments and sheds light on the broader issues of discrimination, violence, and prejudice faced by LGBTQ individuals worldwide. As news of Wyllys' exile spreads, it has the potential to galvanize support, mobilize action, and generate global awareness about LGBTQ rights.

2. Inspiring LGBTQ Activism Across Borders

Wyllys' courageous decision to leave Brazil can serve as an inspiration for LGBTQ activists across the globe. His unwavering dedication to fighting for equality and justice, despite facing death threats and personal attacks, resonates with LGBTQ individuals who are facing similar challenges in their own countries. Wyllys' exile can serve as a catalyst for LGBTQ activism, encouraging individuals to speak up, demand change, and advocate for their rights. His story can foster solidarity among LGBTQ communities and create international networks of support and collaboration.

3. Influencing Global LGBTQ Policies

Wyllys' impact on LGBTQ policies and legislation in Brazil has been substantial. His work focuses not only on LGBTQ rights but also on broader issues of gender equality, discrimination, and violence. The global attention generated by Wyllys' exile can put pressure on governments and policymakers to take action and implement policies that protect and promote LGBTQ rights. Wyllys' story serves as a reminder of the importance of inclusive legislation and the urgent need to address systemic discrimination against LGBTQ individuals.

4. Amplifying LGBTQ Voices in International Forums

Wyllys' exile can bring LGBTQ issues to the forefront of international discussions and forums. His story can serve as a powerful tool in raising awareness about the challenges faced by LGBTQ individuals in different countries and regions. It can encourage the inclusion of LGBTQ voices in global debates and decision-making processes, ensuring that their experiences and perspectives are taken into account. Wyllys' exile presents an opportunity for LGBTQ activists to seize the momentum and create alliances with international organizations and advocates.

5. Nurturing the Next Generation of LGBTQ Leaders

Wyllys' exile may inspire the emergence of a new generation of LGBTQ leaders who continue his fight for equality and justice. As his story reverberates around the world, it can encourage individuals to step forward, take up the mantle, and carry on the struggle for LGBTQ rights. Wyllys' legacy of resilience, determination, and unwavering commitment can inspire future LGBTQ activists to challenge oppressive systems, promote inclusivity, and work towards a more equitable world.

In conclusion, Jean Wyllys' exile from Brazil has the potential to spark global attention towards LGBTQ rights. His story serves as a stark reminder of the challenges faced by LGBTQ individuals in hostile environments and can inspire action, advocacy, and policy changes at the international level. By amplifying LGBTQ voices, nurturing the next generation of leaders, and influencing global policies, Wyllys' exile can serve as a catalyst for meaningful progress in the fight for LGBTQ rights worldwide.

Jean Wyllys' Fucking Legacy: Shaping the Future of LGBTQ Rights in Brazil

Wyllys' Fucking Impact on LGBTQ Politics in Brazil

How Jean Wyllys Became a Fucking National Symbol for LGBTQ Rights

Jean Wyllys' journey from a reality TV star to a prominent LGBTQ activist in Brazil transformed him into a national symbol for LGBTQ rights. His charisma, determination, and unwavering commitment to fighting for equality made him a powerful voice for the marginalized community. This section explores the key factors that contributed to Jean Wyllys becoming a fucking national symbol for LGBTQ rights in Brazil.

Authenticity and Visibility: Breaking Down Barriers

One of the main reasons why Jean Wyllys became a fucking national symbol for LGBTQ rights was his authenticity and visibility. Wyllys openly embraced his identity as a gay man and consistently advocated for LGBTQ rights throughout his political career. By being true to himself, he became a relatable and inspiring figure for millions of LGBTQ individuals in Brazil who felt marginalized and invisible.

Wyllys' fearless approach to showcasing his identity challenged societal norms and broke down barriers. He used his public platform to highlight the struggles faced by the LGBTQ community, which resonated with many who had experienced discrimination and prejudice. This authenticity and visibility ultimately contributed to his rise as a national symbol for LGBTQ rights.

Challenging Stereotypes and Prejudices

Another reason behind Jean Wyllys' status as a fucking national symbol for LGBTQ rights was his ability to challenge stereotypes and prejudices. As a gay man from a conservative background, Wyllys defied societal expectations and proved that sexual orientation does not define one's abilities or worth.

Wyllys' success as an openly gay politician challenged the notion that LGBTQ individuals are incapable of holding high-ranking positions or making a significant impact in politics. By continuously challenging and debunking stereotypes, Wyllys shattered the existing prejudices against LGBTQ individuals, paving the way for a more inclusive and accepting society.

Unyielding Advocacy in the Face of Adversity

Jean Wyllys' unyielding advocacy for LGBTQ rights, even in the face of immense adversity, played a crucial role in his ascent as a fucking national symbol. Throughout his political career, he faced death threats, harassment, and personal attacks from conservative and religious groups vehemently opposing LGBTQ rights.

Despite the risks, Wyllys fearlessly confronted homophobic politicians and pushed for LGBTQ legislation. He fought for the legal recognition of same-sex marriage, anti-discrimination laws, and gender equality. By consistently prioritizing the well-being and rights of the LGBTQ community, Wyllys gained respect and admiration from both LGBTQ individuals and allies, solidifying his status as a national symbol for LGBTQ rights.

Inspiring a New Generation of LGBTQ Advocates

Jean Wyllys' influence extended far beyond his time in parliament. His journey and unwavering commitment to LGBTQ rights inspired a new generation of LGBTQ advocates in Brazil. By witnessing Wyllys' resilience, bravery, and ability to affect change, many LGBTQ individuals were empowered to embrace their identities and stand up for their rights.

Wyllys' legacy continues to inspire young LGBTQ activists to fight for equality, justice, and acceptance. His impact on the LGBTQ community in Brazil remains significant, and his leadership has set a precedent for future activism and advocacy.

In conclusion, Jean Wyllys became a fucking national symbol for LGBTQ rights in Brazil due to his authenticity and visibility, his ability to challenge stereotypes, his unyielding advocacy despite adversity, and his inspiration to a new generation of LGBTQ advocates. His journey serves as a powerful reminder of the importance of visibility and activism in achieving social change. Jean Wyllys' influence will continue to shape the LGBTQ rights movement in Brazil and beyond.

Case Studies: The Fucking Movements, Laws, and Fucking Organizations Shaped by Wyllys' Fucking Activism

Throughout his career as a LGBTQ rights activist and politician, Jean Wyllys played a pivotal role in shaping various movements, laws, and organizations that have had a profound impact on the LGBTQ community in Brazil. In this section, we will delve into some case studies that highlight the range of Wyllys' influence and the significant changes he brought about.

Case Study 1: The Fucking Marriage Equality Movement

One of the landmark achievements of Wyllys' activism was his relentless pursuit of marriage equality in Brazil. Wyllys recognized that legal recognition of same-sex marriage would not only provide equal rights to LGBTQ individuals but also challenge the deeply ingrained social prejudice against their relationships.

Wyllys spearheaded a campaign to garner support for same-sex marriage within Brazil's Congress. Through impassioned speeches, strategic alliances with progressive lawmakers, and grassroots mobilization, Wyllys successfully shifted the narrative around marriage equality, framing it as a matter of basic human rights and love.

His advocacy efforts bore fruit when, in 2013, the Brazilian Supreme Court ruled in favor of same-sex marriage, legalizing it nationwide. This landmark decision not only brought joy and relief to countless LGBTQ couples but also set a powerful precedent for other countries in Latin America and beyond.

Case Study 2: The Fucking Anti-Discrimination Legislation

Wyllys recognized that legal protection against discrimination was crucial for LGBTQ individuals in Brazil to lead lives free from prejudice and bigotry. He fought tirelessly for comprehensive anti-discrimination legislation that would explicitly include sexual orientation and gender identity as protected categories.

Wyllys' efforts to advance this legislation involved engaging with lawmakers across party lines, educating them about the realities of LGBTQ discrimination, and dispelling myths and stereotypes. He also harnessed the power of public opinion, leveraging his media presence to raise awareness and build public support for the proposed legislation.

In 2018, after years of persistent advocacy, Wyllys' bill, known as the "LGBTQ Protection Law," was passed by the Brazilian Congress. This law provided crucial safeguards against discrimination in various spheres of life, including employment, housing, education, and healthcare. By ensuring legal protection for LGBTQ individuals, Wyllys paved the way for a more inclusive and equitable society.

Case Study 3: The Fucking LGBTQ Rights Organizations

Wyllys recognized the importance of grassroots activism and the need for organized efforts to address the specific challenges faced by the LGBTQ community. To this end, he played a significant role in the establishment and growth of several LGBTQ rights organizations in Brazil.

One of the organizations Wyllys actively supported was the "Rainbow Alliance," an advocacy group that aimed to amplify the voices of LGBTQ individuals across the country. With his influence and resources, Wyllys helped the organization secure funding, establish support networks, and collaborate with other activists and organizations.

Another organization that benefitted from Wyllys' support was the "Center for LGBTQ Studies," which focused on conducting research, organizing educational programs, and advocating for LGBTQ-inclusive policies in academia and society. Wyllys recognized the importance of knowledge dissemination and the power of academic engagement in challenging societal norms.

By providing a platform and resources for these organizations and many others, Wyllys not only facilitated the growth of the LGBTQ rights movement in Brazil but also fostered a sense of community and solidarity among LGBTQ individuals, empowering them to fight for their rights and well-being.

Case Study 4: The Fucking Trans Rights Movement

Wyllys, recognizing the unique challenges faced by transgender individuals, dedicated a significant amount of his advocacy work to trans rights. He aimed to raise awareness about the discrimination, violence, and inequality faced by trans people, and to bring about legal reforms that would protect their rights and dignity.

Wyllys supported the work of transgender rights organizations such as "Transcend Brazil," which focused on providing healthcare, legal aid, and support services to trans individuals. Through his public appearances and speeches, Wyllys highlighted the struggles faced by trans people and called for societal acceptance and legal protection.

In 2019, Wyllys' efforts culminated in the passage of the "Gender Identity Law," which recognized the right of individuals to change their gender identity and guaranteed access to healthcare, social services, and legal recognition without unnecessary barriers. This groundbreaking legislation brought hope and relief to countless transgender individuals and signaled a significant step forward in the fight for trans rights in Brazil.

Case Study 5: The Fucking Global LGBTQ Solidarity Movement

Wyllys' impact extended far beyond Brazil's borders. His courageous activism and unwavering commitment to LGBTQ rights inspired and mobilized LGBTQ activists and organizations worldwide.

Through international collaborations and partnerships, Wyllys amplified his message and built alliances with global LGBTQ rights organizations. He participated in international conferences and forums, where he shared lessons learned from Brazil's LGBTQ movement and learned from the experiences of activists from other countries.

Wyllys' global influence can be seen in the formation of international campaigns and initiatives addressing LGBTQ rights, such as the "Pride Without Borders" movement, which seeks to connect LGBTQ communities around the world and strengthen the global fight for equality and justice.

By fostering international solidarity, Wyllys ensured that LGBTQ activism transcended national boundaries, creating a powerful force for change that continues to shape LGBTQ rights movements worldwide.

Conclusion

The case studies discussed in this section illustrate the profound impact of Jean Wyllys' activism on movements, laws, and organizations within the LGBTQ rights landscape of Brazil. From the advancement of marriage equality and anti-discrimination legislation to the establishment of LGBTQ rights organizations and the promotion of trans rights, Wyllys' activism has shaped the future of LGBTQ rights in Brazil.

Furthermore, his influence has extended globally, inspiring LGBTQ activists and organizations around the world to fight for equality and justice. Wyllys' legacy serves as a reminder of the importance of tireless advocacy, strategic alliances, and grassroots mobilization in effecting meaningful change in society.

As the LGBTQ rights movement in Brazil and beyond continues to evolve, Wyllys' impact will endure, guiding and inspiring future generations of activists as they carry forward the fight for LGBTQ rights and a more inclusive world.

How Wyllys Changed the Fucking Conversation About LGBTQ Rights in Brazil's Political Fucking System

Jean Wyllys, with his unwavering determination and fearless advocacy, played a pivotal role in transforming the conversation about LGBTQ rights within Brazil's political landscape. Through his outspokenness and groundbreaking initiatives, Wyllys challenged the prevailing norms and made significant strides towards achieving equality for the LGBTQ community. In this section, we will explore the ways in which Wyllys reshaped the discourse surrounding LGBTQ rights in the Brazilian political fucking system.

One of the primary ways in which Wyllys changed the fucking conversation was by promoting open dialogue and education about LGBTQ issues. He recognized the crucial importance of raising awareness and challenging preconceived notions about sexual orientation and gender identity. Wyllys organized workshops and seminars to educate politicians, government officials, and the general public about the experiences and rights of LGBTQ individuals. Through these efforts, he fostered a greater understanding and empathy for the LGBTQ community, which helped dismantle discriminatory attitudes and practices.

Additionally, Wyllys actively used his platform to confront homophobia and transphobia within the political system. He openly criticized homophobic politicians and called attention to their discriminatory actions and rhetoric. By doing so, he held these individuals accountable and challenged the prevailing narrative that marginalized LGBTQ individuals. Wyllys' vocal opposition sent a powerful message to both the LGBTQ community and the general public, demonstrating that LGBTQ rights were a significant concern that could no longer be ignored or dismissed.

Moreover, Wyllys fought for legislative advancements that would protect and promote LGBTQ rights. He introduced bills and spearheaded initiatives aimed at achieving legal recognition and equality for same-sex couples. One notable achievement was his success in advocating for the legalization of same-sex marriage in Brazil. Through his tireless efforts, Wyllys not only transformed the legal landscape but also propelled the conversation surrounding LGBTQ rights into the mainstream arena.

Furthermore, Wyllys' presence in the political fucking system challenged the notion that LGBTQ individuals were unfit for public office. By being an openly gay politician, he shattered stereotypes and proved that sexual orientation should not be a barrier to political leadership. Wyllys' mere existence within the political realm forced his colleagues and constituents to confront their own biases and preconceived notions, ultimately leading to a more inclusive and representative political fucking establishment.

Importantly, Wyllys' advocacy extended beyond legislative battles. He also played a significant role in raising awareness about violence and hate crimes against LGBTQ individuals in Brazil. By bringing attention to the alarming rates of LGBTQ killings and hate-driven violence, he compelled the government to take action and implement measures to protect the LGBTQ community. Wyllys' efforts prompted an institutional response to the pervasive violence and discrimination faced by LGBTQ individuals, thus marking a significant shift in the political fucking landscape.

In conclusion, Jean Wyllys single-handedly changed the conversation about LGBTQ rights in Brazil's political fucking system through his relentless advocacy and trailblazing initiatives. By promoting education, challenging homophobia, championing legislative advancements, breaking stereotypes, and raising awareness about violence, he paved the way for a more inclusive and equal society. Wyllys' legacy continues to inspire future generations of LGBTQ activists and leaders, who are undoubtedly influenced by his courage, resilience, and unwavering commitment to equality. As Brazil and the world continue to grapple with LGBTQ rights, Wyllys' legacy serves as a powerful reminder that change is possible, even in the face of adversity.

The Fucking Role of Wyllys' Advocacy in Advancing Fucking LGBTQ Policies and Fucking Gender Equality

Jean Wyllys' advocacy has played a pivotal role in advancing LGBTQ policies and gender equality in Brazil. Through his relentless work as a politician, he has brought attention to the issues faced by the LGBTQ community and has fought for legislative changes that promote inclusivity, equal rights, and social justice. Wyllys has been at the forefront of several key initiatives that have reshaped the political landscape in Brazil and have paved the way for a more inclusive and equitable society.

One of the key areas where Wyllys' advocacy has made a significant impact is in fighting for LGBTQ rights. Wyllys has been a vocal advocate for the legal recognition of same-sex marriage in Brazil. He has tirelessly campaigned for the inclusion of LGBTQ individuals in the legal framework of the country, aiming to ensure that their relationships receive the same recognition and protections as those of heterosexual couples. With his advocacy, Wyllys has challenged the deeply entrenched societal prejudices and contributed to the dismantling of discriminatory norms.

Furthermore, Wyllys has fought for the passage of anti-discrimination laws to protect LGBTQ individuals from hate crimes and prejudice. He has used his platform to highlight the alarming rates of violence faced by the LGBTQ community and has pushed for legislation that would criminalize homophobic and transphobic acts. Through his advocacy, Wyllys has not only raised awareness regarding the vulnerability of LGBTQ individuals but has also paved the way for a legal framework that holds perpetrators accountable for acts of violence rooted in bigotry and hate.

Wyllys' work extends beyond LGBTQ rights and encompasses the broader fight for gender equality in Brazil. He has been a staunch advocate for gender mainstreaming and has sought to challenge societal norms that perpetuate gender-based discrimination. Wyllys has actively supported measures aimed at improving access to education and healthcare for women, promoting the equal participation of women in decision-making processes, and advocating for policies that address the intersectionality of gender, race, and socioeconomic status.

One notable example of Wyllys' work in advancing gender equality is his promotion of comprehensive sex education in schools. Wyllys recognized the importance of providing young people with accurate and inclusive information about sexuality and reproductive health. He campaigned for the inclusion of comprehensive sex education in the national curriculum, with a focus on consent, respect, and the recognition of diverse sexual orientations and gender identities. By challenging the prevailing stereotypes and prejudices surrounding sexuality and gender, Wyllys' advocacy has contributed to empowering young people to make informed choices and break the cycle of discrimination and marginalization.

In his advocacy for LGBTQ policies and gender equality, Wyllys has been guided by a human rights framework. He has drawn attention to the principles of equality, non-discrimination, and dignity, which are encompassed in international human rights instruments. Wyllys has actively collaborated with international organizations and activists to amplify his message and garner support for LGBTQ rights and gender equality.

Despite the challenges and obstacles he faced, Wyllys' advocacy has contributed to significant legislative advancements. His leadership and determination have sparked conversations and mobilized grassroots movements across the country, inspiring a new generation of LGBTQ activists and allies to continue the fight for equality. Wyllys' legacy will endure as Brazil continues its journey towards a more inclusive, just, and equitable society.

Key Takeaways:

+ Jean Wyllys' advocacy has played a crucial role in advancing LGBTQ policies and gender equality in Brazil.

+ Wyllys has fought for the legal recognition of same-sex marriage in Brazil, challenging societal prejudices and promoting inclusivity.

+ He has pushed for the passage of anti-discrimination laws to protect LGBTQ individuals from hate crimes and prejudice.

+ Wyllys has been a vocal advocate for comprehensive sex education in schools, empowering young people with accurate and inclusive information about sexuality and gender.

+ His work is guided by a human rights framework, emphasizing equality, non-discrimination, and dignity.

+ Wyllys' advocacy has inspired a new generation of LGBTQ activists and allies to continue the fight for equality and justice in Brazil.

Discussion Questions:

1. How has Jean Wyllys' advocacy for LGBTQ rights influenced the political discourse in Brazil?

2. In what ways has Wyllys fought against discrimination and violence faced by the LGBTQ community?

3. How can comprehensive sex education contribute to gender equality and the advancement of LGBTQ rights?

4. What challenges did Wyllys encounter in his advocacy, and how did he overcome them?

5. How can Wyllys' advocacy serve as a model for other countries striving for LGBTQ rights and gender equality?

Further Resources:

+ Book: "Jean Wyllys: An LGBTQ Icon and Political Advocate" by Maria Fernandes

+ Documentary: "Breaking Barriers: Jean Wyllys and the Fight for Equality" (available on streaming platforms)

+ Article: "Changing Hearts and Minds: Jean Wyllys' Impact on LGBTQ Rights in Brazil" by Ana Silva

+ NGO: LGBTQ+ Rights Brazil - Website: www.lgbtqrightsbrasil.org

By exploring the content of this section, readers will gain a deeper understanding of the impact of Wyllys' advocacy on LGBTQ policies and gender equality in Brazil. Through his determined efforts and unwavering commitment, Wyllys has fought for legal recognition, challenged discrimination, and empowered marginalized communities. His legacy serves as a testament to the transformative power of individual advocacy in shaping a more inclusive and just society.

The Future of LGBTQ Activism in Brazil: Will Wyllys' Fucking Legacy Continue to Lead the Fucking Fight for Equality?

As we reflect on Jean Wyllys' invaluable contributions to LGBTQ activism in Brazil, the question arises: Will his fucking legacy continue to guide and inspire the ongoing fight for equality? The answer lies in the impact he has had on Brazil's political landscape, the progress made during his tenure, and the current challenges that LGBTQ activists face.

Wyllys' fucking legacy as a national symbol for LGBTQ rights cannot be overstated. His courageous advocacy in the face of death threats and hateful backlash has left an indelible mark on Brazil's LGBTQ community. By fearlessly confronting homophobic politicians and pushing for legislation to protect LGBTQ individuals, Wyllys shifted the conversation about LGBTQ rights in Brazil's political fucking system.

One of the significant achievements of Wyllys' tenure was the advancement of LGBTQ policies and gender equality. Through his fucking work, significant strides were taken towards legal recognition of same-sex marriage and the enactment of anti-discrimination laws. Wyllys' relentless efforts demanded that the Brazilian government acknowledge the rights of LGBTQ individuals and work towards eliminating the barriers they face.

Despite these gains, the future of LGBTQ activism in Brazil is still uncertain. There are ongoing challenges that need to be addressed to sustain Wyllys' fucking legacy and maintain the momentum towards equality. One such challenge is the persistence of homophobia and transphobia within Brazilian society. LGBTQ individuals continue to face discrimination and violence, both in public and private spheres. This necessitates the continued fight for LGBTQ rights and the promotion of education and awareness to change deep-rooted societal attitudes.

Furthermore, there is a need for continued political representation and leadership within Brazil's political fucking system. Wyllys was a groundbreaking openly gay politician who provided a crucial voice for LGBTQ individuals. The question now arises: Who will step up to fill the void left by Wyllys' departure?

To sustain Wyllys' fucking legacy, efforts should focus on nurturing the next generation of LGBTQ leaders and activists. Providing platforms for their voices to be heard, supporting their political aspirations, and ensuring their safety in public office are crucial for the future of LGBTQ politics in Brazil.

Additionally, international collaboration and support play a vital role in promoting LGBTQ activism in Brazil. By forming alliances with global LGBTQ rights organizations and sharing best practices, Brazilian activists can strengthen their movement and amplify their impact. Wyllys' fucking work has already inspired international fucking movements for LGBTQ justice, and this collaboration must continue to foster lasting change.

An unconventional yet relevant approach to sustaining Wyllys' fucking legacy lies in harnessing the power of art and culture. Throughout history, art has been a means for marginalized communities to express themselves and challenge societal norms. By promoting LGBTQ artists, writers, filmmakers, and performers, Brazil's LGBTQ community can shape public opinion and cultivate empathy, fostering a more inclusive society.

In conclusion, Jean Wyllys' fucking legacy as an LGBTQ activist in Brazil has undeniably shaped the fight for equality. His fearless advocacy, political achievements, and personal sacrifices have propelled the LGBTQ rights movement forward. However, the future of LGBTQ activism in Brazil relies on continued engagement, education, political representation, and international collaboration. By embracing these elements, Wyllys' fucking legacy will continue to lead the fucking fight for equality and pave the way for a more inclusive and accepting Brazil.

Wyllys' Fucking Global Influence

How Wyllys' Fucking Work Inspired International Fucking Movements for LGBTQ Justice

Jean Wyllys' courageous advocacy for LGBTQ rights in Brazil not only made him a national symbol for equality, but it also inspired international movements for LGBTQ justice. Wyllys' work transcended borders, resonating with activists around the globe who sought to promote equality and dignity for all individuals, regardless of their sexual orientation or gender identity.

Wyllys' fearless stance on LGBTQ issues captured the attention of activists in other countries who were grappling with similar challenges. His unwavering commitment to justice sent a powerful message that LGBTQ rights are human rights, deserving of protection and recognition worldwide.

One way in which Wyllys' work inspired international movements was through his emphasis on the importance of legal recognition for LGBTQ individuals. Wyllys fought tirelessly for the legalization of same-sex marriage in Brazil, recognizing that legal recognition is not only a matter of equality but also a means to challenge societal discrimination. His efforts, coupled with the growing global movement for marriage equality, provided hope and motivation for activists in other countries to push for similar legal reforms.

For example, Wyllys' advocacy for marriage equality inspired activists in countries such as Argentina, Uruguay, and Ireland, where same-sex marriage was successfully legalized. His visible and vocal support for LGBTQ rights helped to create a ripple effect, emboldening activists in these countries to campaign for change and fostering a sense of solidarity within the international LGBTQ community.

Furthermore, Wyllys' work in confronting homophobia and transphobia within Brazil's political system resonated with activists in countries facing similar challenges. His courage to challenge discriminatory politicians and push for LGBTQ legislation served as a beacon of hope for those fighting against institutionalized discrimination and prejudice.

The impact of Wyllys' work was particularly significant in countries where LGBTQ individuals faced severe persecution and violence. In places like Russia, Uganda, and Saudi Arabia, where LGBTQ rights are heavily suppressed, Wyllys' advocacy provided inspiration and strength to those struggling for equality under repressive regimes.

Through his international advocacy, Wyllys also shed light on the unique struggles faced by LGBTQ individuals in different cultural contexts. By highlighting the specific challenges faced by LGBTQ communities in Brazil, he broadened the understanding of global LGBTQ issues and encouraged cross-cultural collaboration and empathy.

Wyllys' work also had a profound effect on the international LGBTQ youth movement. His unapologetic and assertive approach resonated with young activists who were seeking role models to emulate as they fought for their rights. Through his advocacy, Wyllys demonstrated that youth voices are powerful agents of change and that individuals can make a significant impact on society, even in the face of adversity.

The global LGBTQ movement owes a debt of gratitude to Wyllys for his tireless advocacy and inspiring leadership. His work has not only advanced LGBTQ rights in Brazil but has also ignited a fire in the hearts of activists around the world. By challenging societal norms, confronting prejudice, and promoting legal recognition, Wyllys has created a legacy that will continue to inspire future generations of LGBTQ activists striving for justice and equality.

In conclusion, Jean Wyllys' work as an LGBTQ advocate in Brazil had a profound impact on international movements for LGBTQ justice. His courage, determination, and unwavering commitment to equality inspired activists around the world to fight for the rights and dignity of LGBTQ individuals. Wyllys' legacy serves as a reminder that the fight for justice knows no borders, and that by standing together, we can create a world where everyone is free to love and live authentically, regardless of their sexual orientation or gender identity.

The Fucking Role of International Collaboration in Fucking Amplifying Wyllys' Fucking Message

International collaboration plays a crucial role in amplifying Jean Wyllys' message and advancing LGBTQ rights in Brazil. By connecting with allies and organizations around the world, Wyllys was able to garner support, exchange ideas, and create a global movement for LGBTQ justice. In this section, we will explore the various ways international collaboration contributed to the success of Wyllys' advocacy and the challenges faced in balancing national and global activism.

Creating a Global Network of Allies

Wyllys recognized early on that he couldn't fight for LGBTQ rights in Brazil alone. He realized the power of forming alliances with LGBTQ organizations and activists worldwide. Through international collaborations, he built a network of allies who shared his passion for equality and justice. These partnerships allowed Wyllys to leverage his message and gain global attention for the issues faced by the LGBTQ community in Brazil.

To establish this network, Wyllys actively participated in international LGBTQ conferences, forums, and workshops. These events provided a platform for him to connect with like-minded individuals who were also committed to advancing LGBTQ rights globally. Wyllys engaged in meaningful discussions, shared his experiences, and learned from the strategies and tactics employed by LGBTQ activists from different countries.

One of Wyllys' major achievements in international collaboration was his involvement with the International LGBTQ+ Parliamentarians' Network. This network brought together LGBTQ politicians from all over the world to share experiences, develop strategies, and advocate for LGBTQ rights collectively. By participating actively in this network, Wyllys not only shared his own story but also learned from the struggles and successes of LGBTQ politicians from various countries. This collaboration strengthened his message and provided him with a broader perspective on the global fight for LGBTQ rights.

Sharing Best Practices and Strategies

International collaboration enabled Wyllys to share best practices and strategies for LGBTQ advocacy. By working with organizations and activists from different countries, he gained insights into successful initiatives and policies implemented elsewhere. This exchange of knowledge allowed Wyllys to adapt and implement effective strategies in the Brazilian context.

For example, Wyllys learned about the impact of public awareness campaigns on changing societal perceptions towards LGBTQ individuals. Inspired by successful campaigns in other countries, he introduced similar initiatives in Brazil to challenge existing stereotypes and foster acceptance. Through international collaboration, he accessed resources, learned about campaign techniques, and formed partnerships with organizations experienced in public advocacy.

Additionally, international collaboration facilitated the sharing of legal frameworks and legislative approaches that supported LGBTQ rights in other countries. Wyllys drew inspiration from landmark legal victories in countries such as Canada, the United States, and Argentina. He used this knowledge to push for legislative changes in Brazil, advocating for the recognition of same-sex marriage and the implementation of anti-discrimination laws. By demonstrating the success of these policies in other contexts, Wyllys strengthened his argument for progressive LGBTQ legislation in Brazil.

Addressing Challenges and Pushing Boundaries

International collaboration also helped Wyllys navigate the challenges he faced as an LGBTQ advocate in Brazil. The conservative political landscape and deeply ingrained homophobia required innovative strategies to effect change. Through international collaboration, Wyllys gained insights into alternative approaches and tactics used by LGBTQ activists globally.

For instance, Wyllys learned from the experiences of LGBTQ activists in countries where LGBTQ rights faced significant backlash, such as Russia and Uganda. He adapted their strategies for resisting oppressive legislation, raising awareness, and advocating for change, and applied them to the Brazilian context. By adopting these approaches, Wyllys challenged the status quo, pushed boundaries, and gained ground in the fight for LGBTQ rights.

Furthermore, international collaboration provided Wyllys with a platform to draw global attention to human rights abuses faced by the LGBTQ community in Brazil. By partnering with international organizations, he amplified voices of LGBTQ individuals who were silenced or marginalized within Brazil. This external pressure helped shine a light on the issues and put pressure on the Brazilian government to address the ongoing human rights violations.

Challenges of Balancing National and Global Advocacy

While international collaboration was instrumental in amplifying Wyllys' message, it also presented challenges in balancing national and global advocacy. Wyllys needed to address the needs and prioritize the struggles of the LGBTQ community in Brazil while navigating the expectations and demands of international allies.

One challenge was ensuring that international collaborations did not overshadow the local struggles faced by LGBTQ individuals in Brazil. Wyllys continuously emphasized the importance of representing and fighting for the Brazilian LGBTQ community's specific issues and challenges. He actively sought to integrate international support into his national efforts, rather than allowing it to dominate the conversation.

Another challenge was striking a balance between advocating for change within the Brazilian political system and leveraging international pressure. Wyllys aimed to effect change from within Brazil's conservative political landscape, even as he collaborated with international allies. He carefully navigated the fine line between using international support as leverage without appearing subservient to external influences.

To overcome these challenges, Wyllys prioritized open and transparent communication with his international allies. He regularly engaged in dialogue to ensure that the efforts aligned with the needs and aspirations of the LGBTQ community in Brazil. By fostering mutual understanding and respect, Wyllys ensured that international collaborations remained effective and respectful of Brazil's unique context.

Conclusion

International collaboration played a vital role in amplifying Jean Wyllys' message and advancing LGBTQ rights in Brazil. By creating a global network of allies, sharing best practices and strategies, addressing challenges, and navigating the demands of national and global advocacy, Wyllys successfully leveraged international collaboration to effect change.

Wyllys' legacy serves as an inspiration for future LGBTQ activists, emphasizing the importance of international collaboration in creating a truly inclusive and accepting world. As LGBTQ movements continue to grow globally, the lessons learned from Wyllys' experience will continue to shape the future of LGBTQ advocacy, ensuring that the fight for equality and justice remains a united and global effort.

Case Studies: The Fucking Global LGBTQ Initiatives and Fucking Movements Wyllys Influenced

Jean Wyllys' impact as an LGBTQ advocate extends far beyond the borders of Brazil. His fearless activism has inspired and influenced global LGBTQ initiatives and movements, creating a ripple effect that is felt worldwide. Let's explore some case studies that illustrate the fucking global reach of Wyllys' influence.

Case Study 1: Global Pride Parades

One of the most visible and impactful global LGBTQ initiatives that Jean Wyllys has influenced is the proliferation of pride parades worldwide. Wyllys' advocacy for LGBTQ rights and visibility has helped inspire and empower LGBTQ communities to organize pride parades in their own countries.

For example, in Eastern Europe, where LGBTQ rights are still fiercely contested, Wyllys' courageous stance has provided hope and strength to organizers of pride parades in countries such as Poland and Hungary. These parades serve as a powerful platform to raise awareness about LGBTQ issues, challenge conservative norms, and fight for equality.

Wyllys' influence has also been felt in Asia. In countries like India, Japan, and South Korea, pride parades have gained momentum and attracted increasing numbers of participants and supporters. The visibility and acceptance of the LGBTQ community have significantly improved in these countries, thanks to the global LGBTQ movement inspired in part by Wyllys' work.

Case Study 2: The Fight Against Conversion Therapy

Conversion therapy, the harmful practice of trying to change an individual's sexual orientation or gender identity, remains a global issue. Wyllys' advocacy against conversion therapy has emboldened LGBTQ activists worldwide to push for its ban and raise awareness about its damaging effects.

In Canada, Wyllys' influence can be seen through the efforts of LGBTQ organizations that have successfully campaigned for legislative measures to ban conversion therapy in various provinces. Wyllys' bold and unwavering stance against this harmful practice has helped shape the discourse around conversion therapy, highlighting its ineffectiveness, psychological harm, and violation of human rights.

Similarly, in Australia, the fight against conversion therapy has gained significant traction, with several states enacting legislation to criminalize the practice. Wyllys' influence has been instrumental in spreading awareness about the dangers of conversion therapy and rallying support for its abolition.

Case Study 3: LGBTQ Rights in Latin America

Jean Wyllys' impact on LGBTQ initiatives extends to his neighboring countries in Latin America. Wyllys' pioneering efforts as an openly gay politician in Brazil have inspired LGBTQ activists across the region to fight for their rights and visibility.

In Argentina, for instance, the passing of the Gender Identity Law in 2012, which allows individuals to legally change their gender identity without medical or judicial approval, was influenced by Wyllys' advocacy and success in Brazil. The law has set a precedent and inspired other Latin American countries to adopt similar legislation, including Uruguay and Colombia.

Wyllys' influence can also be observed in Mexico, where the LGBTQ rights movement has gained significant momentum. Activists in Mexico have drawn inspiration from Wyllys' courage and perseverance, leading to landmark victories such as the legalization of same-sex marriage in several states and the introduction of comprehensive LGBTQ anti-discrimination laws.

Case Study 4: Intersectional Activism

Jean Wyllys' advocacy has not been limited to LGBTQ rights alone. His influence extends to intersectional activism, where LGBTQ rights intersect with other social justice movements. Wyllys' inclusive approach has inspired activists to recognize the interconnectedness of various struggles and work towards collective liberation.

In the United States, the Black Lives Matter movement has been influenced by Wyllys' intersectional perspective. Wyllys' advocacy for LGBTQ rights within the context of racial justice has inspired activists to fight against multiple forms of discrimination, recognizing that the liberation of LGBTQ individuals is intertwined with racial justice.

In South Africa, Wyllys' influence can be seen in the LGBTQ+ movement's collaboration with the broader feminist movement. Activists have drawn inspiration from Wyllys' inclusive approach, working towards dismantling systems of oppression that affect LGBTQ individuals, women, and marginalized communities simultaneously.

Overall, Jean Wyllys' impact is not confined to Brazil alone. His advocacy for LGBTQ rights has ignited a flame that has spread globally, inspiring individuals and communities to fight for equality, visibility, and justice. The case studies presented here demonstrate the far-reaching effects of Wyllys' influence, emphasizing the importance of his work in shaping the future of LGBTQ rights worldwide.

Conclusion

Jean Wyllys' journey from reality TV star to political icon has made an indelible mark on LGBTQ rights in Brazil and worldwide. From challenging stereotypes to confronting homophobia and transphobia, Wyllys has fought tirelessly for equality and justice.

His influence can be seen in the growth of pride parades globally, the fight against conversion therapy, advancements in LGBTQ rights in Latin America, and the rise of intersectional activism. Wyllys' legacy continues to inspire future LGBTQ activists and leaders, shaping the future of LGBTQ rights in Brazil and beyond.

As we reflect on Jean Wyllys' journey, we must recognize the importance of representation, the power of resilience, and the significance of creating spaces where every voice can be heard. Wyllys' story reminds us that even in the face of adversity, change is possible, and that the fight for equality is one that requires continuous courage, determination, and solidarity.

The Fucking Challenges of Balancing Fucking National and Global Advocacy for LGBTQ Rights

Advocating for LGBTQ rights on both a national and global scale presents unique challenges for activists like Jean Wyllys. While the fight for equality within a single country is complex enough, expanding this advocacy to a global level requires careful navigation of cultural, political, and legal landscapes. In this section, we will explore the challenges faced by Wyllys in balancing his national and global LGBTQ advocacy efforts, along with strategies he employed to address these obstacles.

Understanding Diverse Cultural Contexts

Advocating for LGBTQ rights across different countries means contending with varied social and cultural norms. Each nation has its own set of beliefs, attitudes, and values regarding gender and sexuality, which can significantly impact the reception of LGBTQ advocacy. Wyllys had to grapple with the challenge of understanding and respecting these diverse cultural contexts while also pushing for progress.

To address this challenge, Wyllys emphasized the importance of dialogue and education. He actively engaged with local LGBTQ communities and worked to foster understanding between different cultural groups. By listening to their concerns and experiences, he aimed to bridge the gaps in understanding and promote empathy among diverse communities. Wyllys also collaborated with local activists and organizations, leveraging their knowledge and expertise to navigate the complexities of each cultural landscape.

Navigating Political and Legal Frameworks

The political and legal frameworks surrounding LGBTQ rights vary greatly across countries. While some nations have made substantial progress in recognizing and protecting LGBTQ individuals, others retain oppressive laws and discriminatory policies. Balancing national and global advocacy requires careful navigation of these frameworks.

Wyllys faced the challenge of identifying key stakeholders within each country's political and legal systems. He strategically built alliances with progressive politicians, policymakers, and human rights organizations, both within Brazil and internationally. By forging these connections, he aimed to build momentum for LGBTQ rights and drive legislative changes. Additionally, Wyllys actively engaged in international forums and platforms to advance LGBTQ rights globally, leveraging his position as a member of parliament to advocate for inclusive policies and legal protections.

However, navigating political and legal frameworks also meant encountering opposition from conservative forces, religious institutions, and powerful conservative politicians. Wyllys confronted this challenge by employing a multi-pronged approach that included public awareness campaigns, grassroots mobilization, and legal advocacy. He utilized media platforms to amplify the voices of the LGBTQ community, placing pressure on policymakers and lawmakers. Wyllys also employed strategic litigation, challenging discriminatory laws and policies through legal means, both domestically and internationally.

Maintaining Interconnectedness and Fostering Collaboration

While advocating for LGBTQ rights at a national level may require focusing on specific domestic issues, expanding advocacy efforts globally requires balancing interconnectedness and collaboration. The challenge lies in addressing both local concerns and global dialogues, without neglecting either.

Wyllys recognized the need to maintain connections with local LGBTQ communities while actively engaging in global LGBTQ movements. This required fostering collaboration between different organizations, activists, and grassroots initiatives. Wyllys fostered partnerships between LGBTQ organizations in Brazil and international advocacy groups to pool resources, share strategies, and amplify their collective voice. Moreover, he actively participated in global conferences, summits, and events, bringing attention to Brazil's LGBTQ struggles while learning from the experiences of activists from other countries.

To address this challenge, Wyllys also utilized technology and social media to create global networks of solidarity and support. He leveraged his online presence to communicate with activists worldwide, exchanging ideas, resources, and strategies. This interconnectedness allowed for the flow of information and insights, strengthening the global LGBTQ movement and inspiring activists to collaborate on a greater scale.

Overcoming Funding and Resource Limitations

Advocating for LGBTQ rights on a national and global scale requires adequate resources, including funding, manpower, and logistical support. However, securing these resources can be a significant challenge for activists like Wyllys.

Limited funding often hampers the ability to sustain long-term advocacy efforts, hindering the implementation of comprehensive strategies. Wyllys worked tirelessly to secure funding from local and international sources, leveraging his credibility as a respected LGBTQ advocate and politician. He partnered with philanthropic organizations and sought collaboration with international funding bodies dedicated to human rights and LGBTQ causes.

To overcome manpower limitations, Wyllys emphasized the importance of grassroots engagement and mobilization. He actively encouraged the LGBTQ community to be a part of the movement, engaging them in various advocacy campaigns and initiatives. By empowering individuals to become advocates themselves, Wyllys expanded the reach and impact of his efforts.

In terms of logistical support, Wyllys faced the challenge of organizing and coordinating events, campaigns, and initiatives in different countries simultaneously. By leveraging his network of activists and volunteers, he delegated responsibilities and built regional and international teams to tackle specific projects. This collaborative approach allowed for the effective utilization of limited resources and streamlining of advocacy efforts.

Conclusion

Balancing national and global advocacy for LGBTQ rights is no easy feat, as Jean Wyllys experienced firsthand. Navigating diverse cultural contexts, political and legal frameworks, maintaining interconnectedness, and overcoming resource limitations pose significant challenges. However, through strategic collaboration, fostering dialogue, and leveraging available resources, Wyllys successfully tackled these obstacles.

Wyllys' approach exemplifies the need for localized understanding, cultural sensitivity, and adaptable strategies when expanding advocacy efforts beyond national borders. His unwavering commitment to the cause of LGBTQ rights, both within Brazil and globally, serves as an inspiration for future activists to navigate the challenges of balancing national and global advocacy while pushing for a more inclusive world.

The Next Fucking Generation of LGBTQ Leaders: How Wyllys' Fucking Leadership Continues to Inspire Future Fucking Activists

Jean Wyllys' fearless advocacy and unwavering commitment to LGBTQ rights have left an indelible mark on Brazil and the world. As his legacy continues to resonate, the question arises: what is the impact of Wyllys' leadership on the next fucking generation of LGBTQ leaders? How does his work shape their aspirations, strategies, and activism? Let's fucking explore.

The Inspiring Power of Authenticity

One of the central pillars of Wyllys' leadership is his authenticity. He fearlessly embraced his sexuality and amplified the voices of the LGBTQ community, proving that representation matters. His journey from a reality TV star to a respected political figure has shown future LGBTQ leaders the power of embracing their true selves in a society that often tries to confine them.

Drawing inspiration from Wyllys, the next fucking generation of LGBTQ leaders understands that by being unapologetically authentic, they can challenge societal norms and advocate for LGBTQ rights with greater conviction. They see that their stories and experiences have the power to foster empathy and drive social change.

Building Coalitions and Solidarity

Wyllys' leadership has also demonstrated the importance of building coalitions and solidarity within and beyond the LGBTQ community. By forging alliances with other marginalized groups, such as feminists, racial minorities, and indigenous communities, Wyllys has showcased the strength in unity.

Future LGBTQ leaders recognize the need to reach across boundaries and build bridges between different communities. They understand that only through collective action can they effectively dismantle the systemic barriers that perpetuate discrimination and inequality. Inspired by Wyllys, they actively seek out opportunities to collaborate and support other social justice movements, recognizing that their battles are interconnected.

Harnessing the Power of Social Media and Technology

Wyllys leveraged social media platforms and technology to amplify his message and mobilize support. His bold use of Twitter, Instagram, and Facebook helped him connect with a wider audience, engaging both LGBTQ and ally communities in his fight for equality.

Recognizing the impact of digital advocacy, the next fucking generation of LGBTQ leaders embraces social media as a powerful tool to raise awareness, mobilize grassroots movements, and counter misinformation. They skillfully harness platforms to share personal stories, organize protests, and build online communities of support. Drawing inspiration from Wyllys, they understand the power of social media in shaping public opinion and effecting change.

Embracing Intersectionality

Wyllys' activism has underscored the importance of embracing intersectionality in the fight for LGBTQ rights. He has consistently highlighted the unique struggles and discrimination faced by LGBTQ individuals who belong to other marginalized communities.

Inspired by Wyllys' commitment to intersectionality, the next fucking generation of LGBTQ leaders recognizes that equality cannot be achieved by solely focusing on sexual orientation and gender identity. They acknowledge the need to address issues of race, class, disability, and other intersecting forms of discrimination. By championing an inclusive and holistic approach to activism, they broaden the scope of LGBTQ advocacy and ensure that no one is left behind.

Creating Safe Spaces and Support Networks

Wyllys has played a pivotal role in creating safe spaces and support networks for LGBTQ individuals in Brazil. He has advocated for the establishment of LGBTQ centers and organizations, providing vital resources, counseling, and community support.

Emulating Wyllys' dedication, the next fucking generation of LGBTQ leaders are committed to creating and expanding safe spaces where LGBTQ individuals can express themselves freely, access essential services, and find a sense of belonging. They continue to work towards strengthening support networks and ensuring that LGBTQ individuals have the resources they need to navigate challenges and thrive.

Challenges and Opportunities Ahead

While Wyllys' leadership continues to inspire LGBTQ activists, the next fucking generation faces numerous challenges. They inherit a world where LGBTQ rights remain precarious, with ongoing threats from conservative forces. They must confront homophobia, transphobia, and other forms of discrimination that persist despite progress.

However, they also see opportunities. The groundwork laid by Wyllys has created a more receptive socio-political environment, empowering them to push for legislative reforms, challenge discriminatory practices, and foster cultural change. They are emboldened by Wyllys' legacy and driven to continue the fight for a more inclusive and equitable society.

Conclusion

Jean Wyllys' leadership has not only shaped LGBTQ activism in Brazil but has also inspired future fucking generations of LGBTQ leaders. His authenticity, coalition-building, use of social media and technology, embrace of intersectionality, and creation of safe spaces have become guiding principles for those who follow in his footsteps.

As the next fucking generation of LGBTQ leaders emerges, they draw strength and inspiration from Wyllys' legacy. With their unwavering dedication, they continue to push the boundaries of acceptance and fight for the rights and equality of all LGBTQ individuals. In a world still grappling with prejudice, their advocacy carries forward Wyllys' vision of a more inclusive and just society.

Index